BOWLING GREEN STATE UNIVERSITY

DISCARDED

LIBRARY

What *Else* You Can Do With a Ph.D.

This book is dedicated to all those people who are using their doctoral experience and extraordinary talents to create exciting, fulfilling careers in the world of commerce.

—Jan Secrist

I dedicate this book to all doctoral graduates who recognize, appreciate, and utilize their numerous skills to find happiness in their careers, wherever their paths may lead.

—Jacqueline Fitzpatrck

What Else You Can Do With a Ph.D.

A CAREER GUIDE FOR SCHOLARS

JAN SECRIST
JACQUELINE FITZPATRICK

Sage Publications, Inc.
International Educational and Professional Publisher
Thousand Oaks ■ London ■ New Delhi

Copyright © 2001 by Sage Publications, Inc.

All rights reserved. No part of this book may be reproduced or utilized in any form or by any means, electronic or mechanical, including photocopying, recording, or by any information storage and retrieval system, without permission in writing from the publisher.

For information:

Sage Publications, Inc.
2455 Teller Road
Thousand Oaks, California 91320
E-mail: order@sagepub.com

Sage Publications Ltd.
6 Bonhill Street
London EC2A 4PU
United Kingdom

Sage Publications India Pvt. Ltd.
M-32 Market
Greater Kailash I
New Delhi 110 048 India

Printed in the United States of America

Library of Congress Cataloging-in-Publication Data

Secrist, Jan.
  What else you can do with a Ph.D.: A career guide for scholars / by
Jan Secrist, Jacqueline Fitzpatrick.
    p. cm.
Includes bibliographical references and index.
  ISBN 0-7619-1969-4 (hc: acid-free) — ISBN 0-7619-1970-8
(pb: acid-free)
  1. Vocational guidance—United States. 2. College
graduates—Employment—United States. 3. Occupations—United States.
I. Fitzpatrick, Jacqueline. II. Title.
  HF5382.5.U5 S425 2000
  331.7'02325'0973—dc21   00-009520

01   02   03   10   9   8   7   6   5   4   3   2   1

Acquiring Editor:	Marquita Flemming
Editorial Assistant:	MaryAnn Vail
Production Editor:	Diana E. Axelsen
Editorial Assistant:	Victoria Cheng
Typesetter/Designer:	Barbara Burkholder
Indexer:	Mary Mortensen
Cover Designer:	Michelle Lee

Contents

Part II

Part III

Part IV

Acknowledgments

Many thanks to Harry Briggs, our first editor, for his enthusiastic support of this idea and his frequent helpful suggestions in research and structure, and to Marquita Flemming, our new editor, whose enthusiasm, rapid e-mail responses, and bright ideas pulled the pieces together with speed and efficiency. To the rest of the Sage staff: Thanks for being such a great team.

A special thank-you to the many individuals who willingly shared your stories, frustrations, dreams, and successes. Although many of you chose to remain anonymous, we deeply appreciate your contributions to this effort. It would not have come together without you.

A round of applause is in order for our husbands and families who urged us on while keeping us balanced in the Real World. It's a wonderful place to live and work.

Introduction

Dear Dr. Hopeful:

We are impressed with your extensive academic credentials but regret to inform you that there are no tenured positions available at our university. We wish you success in your academic search.

Sincerely,
A Happily Tenured Dean

Have you received a few of these form letters? Or have you heard the sad tales from those who have a stack of them? There are not enough openings for all tenure-track hopefuls today, and there haven't been since the 1960s, when multitudes of newly minted professors were hired with the implied promise of lifetime employment. Many 1990s graduates figured that after 30 years, those professors would be skipping off to less-demanding scholarly pastures or green golf courses, and tenured positions would be opening up just in time for them.

Solid thinking, but it doesn't account for major financial and institutional changes. Once mandatory retirement ages were abolished, many entrenched professors decided to remain in their book-lined offices. Budgetary constraints pushed universities to hire temporary professors in adjunct form—which means huge cost savings because benefits are rarely included with temporary positions. We have read in alumni magazines and quotations in national magazines by college career centers that only half the teaching positions in universities today are tenure track, and that number is expected to continue to decline. We've read that the current national average is that actually less than 30% of tenure track applicants have a chance of being hired. What a discouraging picture.

The *Chronicle of Higher Education* reported in 1999 that a total of 44,652 new doctorates were handed out in 1995-1996 (the latest figures available), with 21,116 of those in the fields of social sciences, health care, ethnic and multidisciplinary, and communication-related studies. Many of these new graduates have sought temporary positions in universities hoping eventually to be considered for full-time work, with goals of someday landing squarely on the elusive tenure track.

For these adjuncts, however, a future in academia is not a rosy picture. They often are expected to teach a full semester course for as little as $1,500 per semester, which is what most tenured professors make in one week, or they get only partial class assignments that can be eliminated on a departmental whim. Many instructors complain that just as they get to know the students and develop working relationships, they are ushered out to await a summons for another semester. It's job insecurity in capital letters.

One extremely qualified candidate spent several years straddling the adjunct path and a tenured-professorship-seeking path before creating her own career as a full-time writer. She stated,

> The junior professors I knew were uniformly overworked, insecure, and unhappy. The stability of tenure grows ever more elusive, even as both teaching loads and the requirements to publish become heavier. At the same time, publishers are cutting their book lists, increasing the shark-like frenzy of academia's "publish or perish" atmosphere.

Her follow-up writing revealed the depth of her frustrations. "When I think of the institution of academia, anger, disappointment, and a sense of betrayal wash through me."

Some of these new docs move to the high school level, public or private, where they willingly scale down academically in return for not living under the publish-or-perish dictum. They feel their degree is respected instead of just being another doctorate among many. And they get summers off, which for many is a chance to pursue their own intellectual interests, or write, or work another part-time job.

For those whose hearts are set on tenure track, however, there is another hurdle to consider. We'd like to share a story of a superbly qualified young woman who found that one of the many reasons tenured positions are becoming so scarce—a reason often undiscovered unless one is immersed in the search process—is the quietly changing competitive field. Jennifer

Carrell, Ph.D. from Harvard (B.A. Stanford, M.A. Oxford), told us that in her extensive job search for a tenured position, she continually encountered (among other frustrations) the situation in which many associate professors from large universities

> are moving sideways—they are jumping off tenured ladders because there is no room for upward movement [at their university], and are willing to go to state universities or smaller colleges and begin again as an assistant professor, to be on a ladder that has real steps upward. So the competition pool ranges from new graduates, out of school 2 to 3 years, to associate professors from other schools with two or three books published. Who can compete with that?

Apparently, not many.

Time magazine confirmed what Jennifer told us in a series called "Arts and Sciences: The New Wave," quoting statistics from the American Psychological Association that outline pay scales, hot jobs, gender shifts, and declining percentages of Ph.D.s in different areas (if you are interested in numbers, even more current statistics are available on the Internet and in almost any magazine related to education you can find).

We all know what those with science and math doctorates have done for many years: leaped out of the Ivory Tower into lucrative and satisfying careers in business, research, and industry. Their skills are eminently transferable, and they know it. The computer world alone is reveling in this brain power and training.

But what is one to do with a communication, history, psychology (by far the largest degree pool), sociology, or English doctorate if teaching is not available? The range, believe it or not, is wide open, limited only by your imagination. You have remarkable and exciting skills. You need only to broaden your search for productive careers. Some new docs are heading into publishing, research, public relations, sales and/or marketing, advertising, or arts and entertainment. Others find themselves in law enforcement, think tanks, policy-making departments of all sizes, library sciences, health care, or the transportation industries. A few are entrepreneurs, writers, or working in local and city governments. And this is only a smattering of potential areas of employment. It's the skill list that's important, not always the industry itself. Every arena needs talented, hard-working employees.

This volume will increase your confidence and help you position yourself for the energetic business world, also known as "the real world." You may even be able to pay off your school loans in far fewer years than you imagined. You will meet many new and exciting people who are free to exercise their creative streaks and know which battles are important and which need to be ignored. And, unless you go into research, you will not have to add footnotes to all your future writings!

We wrote this book because we found ourselves, along with many fellow graduates, going through a challenging process: proud of our doctoral degrees yet increasingly disappointed by finding only adjunct openings in academia. We eventually asked ourselves, "What now?" Jacque found her evaluation, critical thinking, and teaching skills were valuable in her supervising of student teachers; Jan bounded out into the business world using her flexible organizational, written, and verbal communication skills while conducting career transition seminars for companies in many different industries. We kept our ears to the ground and maintained a deep curiosity about how people reevaluate and prioritize when forced to choose new goals. After some fascinating interviews exposing discouraging hiring trends, we dug deeper and decided to put this material into book form.

We feel this material will help you clarify the many skills used in academia that can now be successfully applied to the industry that best matches your talents and goals. All those presentations you made during the doctoral program, all the reading you struggled through and the knowledge you have absorbed, the marvelous writing skills in which you excelled, even your time management skills, will be enhanced with new freedom of expression.

We have chosen camera lenses as a picturesque (pun intended) metaphor for a book discussing the academic challenges you have just survived and the commerce goals you now seek. We are not talking about the point-and-shoot cameras that simply see the world as it is, neatly framed with natural lighting and no questions asked, just push one button and out pops a flat facsimile. (Remind you of some classes?) We are talking about a high-tech camera with interchangeable lenses, allowing you to create a wide range of creative options that bring you the greatest personal and professional rewards.

We start with a portrait lens, which focuses on one small close-up and blurs the rest of the world. You will turn the camera on yourself first; you are the close-up. It is important to have an evaluation and understanding of individual personality and goals so you can showcase your complete album of talents and skills in the best possible light. Then you gradually will change to a lens that broadens your perspective and brings more details into closer range. The middle sections of this book offer the broadening perspective as you begin your job search in earnest. Toward the end, we return to a portrait lens to encourage you to take full responsibility for making job decisions based on your personal values, goals, interests, and skills.

Professional photographers will tell you they are pleased to get one or two good photos out of a roll of 36 exposures. That is exactly what you will be aiming for: shooting for as many possibilities as possible, and probably firing off several rolls of résumés. But you will be delighted (that's the plan anyway) when one or two excellent job offers come back to you in an environment that fits your talents, interests, and goals.

Now it's time to put in a fresh roll of film. Say goodbye to academic jargon, critical or supercompetitive fellow students, small or no paychecks, and drowsy audiences as you load fresh film and aim your camera toward whatever profession you choose. Give thanks to academia for sharpening your reasoning, writing, and thinking skills, and then create your own portfolio.

You'll create a sparkling, new, clearly focused portrait in less time than you can imagine.

PART I

CHAPTER 1

Assessing Your Academic Powers

The Gifts of Knowledge

Throughout your academic career, you have worn many hats; some were official, some burst forth out of financial necessity, and a few others probably were created to feed your dreams. You obviously have been a student; you also may have been a teacher, aide, employee, adviser, researcher, graduate fellow, freelance writer, library hound, or computer wizard. You may even have been an unofficial counselor, curriculum adviser, or class clown.

For now, however, we would like you to think of yourself as a photographer. Not as the owner of one of the popular, pocket-sized "point-and-shoot" cameras (also known as p.h.d. cameras, standing for "push-here-dummy") but as a photographer with an impressive and varied set of lenses and the ability to focus, zoom, frame, and click the shutter at your chosen aperture and speed. Because that is what we will be doing in this book, encouraging you to use every lens and photographic tool and trick of lighting in your camera bag as you examine who you are, where you want to go, and how to get there.

For the duration of your academic travels, you have used a wide-angle lens, aiming at every related book, every Internet-accessible library in your town or anyone else's, and any piece of research or literature that would help you focus on your goals. You may even have collared individuals from near and far who could help clarify the picture of how you could achieve that "terminal" (some choice of words, huh?) degree.

That lens has served you well. For now, however, we would like you to dust it off carefully and return it to your gadget bag, because to begin the job search process, it is important to change your customary subject. For now, you need to use a portrait lens and turn the camera on yourself. No fair using soft filters that hide the wrinkles and warts and fatigue marks and bags under the eyes. This lens needs to be in sharp focus, giving great detail of who you are, with only the background softly blurred. It is your turn to be the subject as you examine your talents, skills, and the powers that brought you this far (for suggested readings on the topics of this and all the chapters, see Appendix A).

The process of doctoral study requires the development of many skills, some of which you can reel off without pausing for breath. Others may have to be teased out and reexamined to be believed. The value of focusing on these gifts of knowledge is twofold: First, we want you to stop concentrating (for a short time) on the work you have completed, or almost completed, and second, we would like to encourage you to evaluate and articulate your many skills. Some of these talents are immediately evident: Biologists often are recruited by the pharmaceutical or biotech industries; English graduates abound in the public relations, advertising, and publishing fields. But there are many other opportunities in the "real world" for the rest of us.

If you know you will be leaving academia, as many new graduates are being forced to do, you probably have agonized over this decision. Teaching may be your passion and, until now, your only interest, but this is the time to be realistic. Although many people cringe at the thought of leaving ivory towers, they need to understand clearly how shrinking tenured opportunities at the university level limit their academic future.

The current academic trend to hire part-time instructors—who tend to be given the less popular classes and who have little prestige, decision-making power, job security, and an unknown future—is an economic reality. Another downer for adjuncts is, as one woman said, "It's lonely; there's no one to brainstorm and share ideas with. I didn't know other professors in my own department, much less at other institutions." The academic world that offers tenured, progressively responsible, prestigious positions is becoming like that blurry old photo of your favorite fun-loving aunt you have tucked away in an album. The relationship was great while it lasted, but the world is different now. Your aunt is long gone, and so is that dream for many graduates.

Clearly, you cannot change the fluctuating trends of academia; all you can do is focus on yourself. First, point the zoom lens inward to capture a more detailed self-portrait: Know yourself, your interests, abilities, and gifts of knowledge that you take—cheerfully and confidently, we hope—into the world of commerce. (*Commerce* and *industry* are terms used in this book to refer to all positions outside academia, including those in government, health care, healing and creative arts, nonprofits, and any other venture you can dream up for yourself.)

If academia has been a lifetime dream of yours, as it seems to be for so many doctoral students and graduates, it is a dream that causes pain as it drifts off into the distance. Giving up a cherished goal is never easy and often takes some fancy mental adjustments. You may find yourself talking to as many people as you can find, moaning, complaining, even getting teary or angry at the prospect of having to make such a big change. Know that this is normal, but also know that you, like so many before you and many more to come, will conquer the same challenges with success. Your talents are many; your skills are fine-tuned and vitally needed.

Doctoral studies require certain skills that can be applied to real-world environments. Many doctoral graduates (especially those who have toiled in the ivory tower full-time) fail to recognize that they have many useful, even essential skills for many jobs outside academia. Those possessing finely tuned "habits of the mind" have a distinct advantage over others applying for the same positions.

The obvious skills, which should be announced in bold letters, are writing, research, critical analysis (the foundation of any successful graduate student), and time management. If, however, you took 14 years to complete the program, please do not brag about your time management talents, unless you have an airtight Rip Van Winkle excuse.

But let's not stop yet. There are many additional skills that are widely appreciated outside the academy, including investigative and organizational skills, public speaking, handling pressure situations (comprehensives seem to stick in our minds), and intuition (remember trying to guess answers on your qualifying exams?). If you wrote a qualitative dissertation, you have finely tuned interview skills that offered you greater insights. Add to this picture the challenges of the fast-paced technology world, and know that your ability to amass large amounts of information and successfully apply that information to the task at hand is a skill that most, if not all, businesses appreciate and seek. Your self-portrait is looking better all the time.

Perhaps the greatest gift you have is the desire and ability to learn, and learning is something you will continue to do because it is who you are, whether you apply your skills in academia or in the wide world of industry. Where and how you decide to apply this skill to a work environment is up to you. Of course, you may be so ready for a rest that you may take a few weeks off and stroll through your town wearing the T-shirt we saw recently, "Will not work for *anything*."

If those doctoral initials after your name are scarcely dry around the edges, you may be fresh enough to the job-seeking process to need a cold reminder: Some businesspeople are uneasy being with folks whose extra initials represent recently acquired doctorates. You may get a silent stare or an occasional startled "Ohhh, wow" reaction. Other people—usually in the interview process—will blithely announce that you are overqualified for the position, because, frankly, they are intimidated by your credentials (although they will not admit it). The same reaction can occur in academia: "Can you imagine a tenured professor at Berkeley being intimidated by my credentials?" one job seeker asked. It happens everywhere, in the ivory tower and in industry.

Writing and Editing

Let's focus on the most obvious in your album of skills that is appreciated by practically every potential employer today—the ability to write. "Well, duhhh," you might mumble, assuming this is a talent that is well-honed in every college-educated or semieducated brain. Not so, not so. We discovered in our teaching adventures that many universities allow their students to graduate without writing a research paper. We have interviewed students from several large universities in different states (which, of course, shall remain nameless in the interest of our health and safety) who stated with obvious pride, "I found all the courses I needed to graduate without writing a single research paper." In our astonishment, we conducted a mini-research study and discovered there were other students lurking in graduate classes or surviving happily in the real world with nary a writing course in their résumé or brain bank. The ability to write well is not a skill to be taken lightly.

As a doctoral student/graduate, you simply cannot escape the experience of writing. In fact, you probably reveled in the creative process. Clearly, you are academically inclined and would not even conceive of, much less search for, classes without writing assignments. As one of our colleagues admitted, "Writing has gotten me into—and out of—so many interesting or difficult situations, I simply cannot imagine a life without it." No serious doctoral student can imagine a life without writing. You may have been one of those students who sought every possible class that encouraged writing skills. You probably loved to express yourself with papers and exams, and you may have even counted the doctoral semesters until you could finally "write your own stuff" in the dissertation process. Of course, you had to write it in a prescribed and time-honored manner, with particular sequence, style, and organization, and you may even have had committee members challenging each other for the final choice of wording, so you were not completely free. But at least you could finally write.

And so we learn to write . . . even if one of you reading this book was the exception who slipped through the cracks in the undergraduate years without writing anything significant. Once you moved into the graduate ranks, we are sure you became strong, solid writers for survival and maybe even grew to love the game of word-smithing.

Now for the good news: The love of proper English usage and joy in writing are much appreciated and often sought-for talents. Writing with clarity is a skill. Many in academia, however, have been rightly accused of writing in the abstract, with run-on sentences that may span several pages, using a multisyllabic vocabulary that stuns and silences the "typical working person" (whomever that may be). We think of this as an oversized, fuzzy landscape photo with a few sharp details but a confusing composition.

If you can shake the fuzzy stuff, the business world will love you and hire you and give you many writing assignments—especially if you demonstrate your love of short, clear, concise English. (Other languages apply here as well.) All your writing skills will be valued, with the exception of one aspect: Lose the long-windedness that served you well in the dissertation. If you are comfortable and clever in the art of editing and revising, you easily will produce the tight, vigorous writing that is highly valued in the real world.

For many, this is the most difficult school-to-commerce transition of all. Editing is something many writers try to avoid; some feel changing their creative musings is akin to poking fiery matches under their fingernails; others are loathe to change a word, a comma, a sentence, much less a paragraph or page. But editing is vital, and although you may not love it, you are probably much better at it than you realize.

Remember Mark Twain's famous line about thanking God every day for making him a writer instead of an editor? Well, no such luck for those of us who survived a doctoral program; we have no hope of emulating Twain's philosophy. We have to do it all. We write, we edit. We create, we compact. We ramble, we revise. We turn a lovely phrase one day; we toss it out the next. Some of us revel in this process.

When researching positions in the business world, you will be glad you know how to edit and rewrite, because time is a critical commodity. Endless editing is a luxury when facing inflexible deadlines. The business world is notorious for the saying "Time is money" (even if that is not structurally correct). The good part, however, is that we also do not have professorial people examining every word, challenging thought processes, perhaps even inserting his or her own words into our fresh, creative ideas. Instead, we have bottom-line bosses pointing to the wall clock and urging completion of that business article/report/survey/manual or current assignment. Your strong talents of creativity, research skills, a writing style, and ability to use everyday vocabulary will help you both on your job application and in your future position.

Research Skills

We keep mentioning research skills because they were such an integral part of your education, yet many of us forget to tout this talent when we are in the job market. Of course you have terrific talents: Your completed (or soon-to-be) dissertation is proof of that. Remember the phrase often tossed about early in your doctoral program that when you complete the extensive classwork (survival is implied, but not promised), you will embark on a dissertation? Remember the definition of a *dissertation:* "An original project including clarification of a problem through extensive use of research with a conclusion drawn from the research and related work." (This definition should impress some interviewers!) At the end of the dissertation process, we typically are focused on our findings and not the previous research. But the hours of research provided us with vigorous words, a powerful message, and a talent that the major portion of our population will never experience. You have a distinct advantage when showcasing these transferable skills.

The process of conducting research is being redefined by computer technology, and current students must be overjoyed by being able to find almost any information available, in virtually any library in the world, simply by knowing the right words to type into their search engine. Sometimes, we can zero in on the exact information needed and can produce a perfect answer to a thorny problem.

At other times, we are surprised by time-consuming searches that may wander into areas not originally intended: Some are hilarious, some are not the least bit funny, and a few are excitingly productive. We have found that some of these unexpected backdoor approaches can lead to elusive and prized kernels of information. No matter the process, you do know how to track down vital information.

Excellent research skills may be the centerpiece of this photograph, but lurking around the edges are several other implied skills, the clearest of which is the ability to work independently. This is an increasingly coveted and sought-after business skill. If we did not have this talent before grad school, we certainly developed it quickly. We learned the value of independence the first day of classes when given a five-page syllabus with no one willing to guide us through the details. Nor was there anyone hanging over us in the library, on the computer, or when teaching undergraduates. Knowing how to work efficiently and alone is a doctoral trademark, and, depending on your chosen career, it may be a critical talent in your future. (Others have it as well, of course—this is hardly an exclusive arena—but it is a required attribute for serious graduate work.)

You will not always have a computer on hand, but that will not deter your research skills. The old-fashioned methods of sitting on well-trod library floors, selecting tomes with catchy titles, and blowing dust off tired bindings are still used and enjoyed by many students. We can easily scour a table of contents or the index and know quickly if the book is a keeper or gets tossed on the reshelving cart. This time-honored research style may not be in your future in a business environment, depending on the area of information you are seeking, of course, but the ability to know your way around a library is a valuable skill for anyone.

Critical Analysis

Responsible jobs require critical analysis, and you have this talent in abundance. How would management function without the ability to analyze situations, articulate requirements, prioritize positions, make workable plans, and settle on solid decisions? You will find yourself appreciating those professors who forced you to consider various sides of an issue while assessing those sometimes tedious books. They were giving your brain good exercises. Whether you agreed or disagreed with the position, you eventually understood a multisided problem and had clarified your own core beliefs on any given issue.

Listening to others, reading, studying information, and analyzing how that information can be applied in the business world is important for many positions, from office workers to supervisors to management to CEOs. We may be entering a more involved technical world, but businesses still need people to listen to colleagues working in the same offices, to clients who try to explain their needs, to competitors who possess other strengths. These different points of view then must be analyzed, positions must be clarified, and decisions must be made.

The ability to state one's view with clarity is a huge time-saver and a valued commodity. You should be good at this, you have years of experience with limited-time exams in which you had to sell your ideas quickly, smoothly, and articulately to the professor. We always had more information than time (for some of the courses) and were forced to condense our vast knowledge into a few paragraphs. The business world is no different: Simply impress your boss instead of the faculty. Furthermore, there is an advantage: Bosses pay for this talent, and some even offer bonuses and job promotions along with regular pay hikes and other perks.

Critical analysis skills can be applied to any segment of the working world, from research to consulting to creating to directing others. They will add credibility to your own working patterns as well as to those of others in almost any working situation. Although the mere presence of those important initials after your name implies you can think and analyze and synthesize information, this is still an area worthy of your bragging.

It can work for you in other areas, as well. If you have an unadvertised talent for stalling an issue, beating around the bush, or inventing wild scenarios that give the impression you know exactly what you were talking about, that's fine. Much of the real world operates on the give-an-opinion-now-and-do-the-analysis-later philosophy. And if you have to change your story, you are probably good at this, too. Sounds like the Nike ad: Just Do It.

Time Management

Let's face it: Time management was forced on us when we made the decision to pursue higher education with the goal of an eventual graduation. We know from the first day of class—indeed, from the initial orientation—how many weeks the classes last, how many semesters are required to complete course work, and how many chapters will (probably) be in the dissertation. If teaching, we know how much material to cram into the semester, and we rely on the dean's memos to tell us exactly when to schedule exams and turn in final grades. We even manage flexible office hours for students panicked about their grades. Juggling all those tiny details and responsibilities will come in handy wherever you land.

Many graduate students have found creative ways to schedule appointments with themselves, allowing occasional free time for lounging at the movies and squeezing fun times in with work times. You do not have to brag about your time management skills—they are implied by your degree—but it never hurts to be aware of their importance.

Investigative Skills

Doctoral students have an abundance of curiosity, or they would not tackle such a huge challenge. Curiosity sharpens our investigative skills, for we know that many paths will be like blank rolls of film: They simply will not contain any information. But we are going to keep clicking that shutter for more pictures, because we have the determination to keep going until we find the answer. Logic does not always apply when talking about detective talents; in fact, the willingness to abandon logic and open our minds to any possibility is a key component.

Investigative skills may require people skills, hard data gathering, or creative methodology, but you know how to go after what you need, even if you must keep digging to negotiate sudden detours. It is a skill highly valued in most business environments, mainly because the world's information systems are increasing faster than anyone can follow, and no one can claim to be an expert at everything anymore. Just as you tracked down research subjects, or sifted through piles of data, you will probably find yourself using similar skills in whatever work you do. Those who are savvy at conducting research on the Internet, the newest and perhaps most comprehensive resource, will have even more successful investigative skills. If you possess excellent people skills, you will know whom to interview and how to follow through on leads, all of which will be an asset in any venture you undertake.

Organizational Skills

When all the paths have been examined, the material gathered, printed, and mixed with notes and scribbles scattered over your desk, you will silently bless the wonderful organizational skills that have been finely honed during undergrad, master's, and doctoral studies. Knowing, almost instinctively, how to tell the story you are about to create is truly a gift of knowledge. You fine-tuned this talent in preparing and giving lectures, seminars, and workshops. As you prepared the material, you practiced the art of storytelling, planning a catchy beginning, a strong story, and a make-'em-think ending. Every time you made a presentation, worked on a project, or organized a weekend seminar or workshop, you knew, with each incoming group, that the students were becoming more sophisticated about the world and its offerings, so your organizational skills probably improved with each group. Being well organized may be second nature to you. It certainly is a talent and a gift to be treasured and touted.

Public Speaking—aka Polished Presentations

"My doctoral work required many presentations," said a current full-time researcher, "varying from 20 minutes to 2 hours. I was critiqued and graded on my delivery skills, yet I was never once given any help, suggestions, or encouragement on my presentation skills." It reminded him of the dunking booth in a high school carnival: Stand on the stool and get knocked into the water, over and over again.

Presentations are an important part of doctoral work and will most likely become a powerful attribute for your future work. From course work to teaching assignments to the all-stressful doctoral defense, you had to stand up in front of a group and appear knowledgeable. What were the characteristics that contributed to a successful delivery?

Preparation tops the list. Teaching requires a great deal of advance work. You may be blessed with a brilliant brain stuffed to the lid with facts, like a Nikon camera with more accessories and gadgets than you will ever figure out, but that does not mean you can sell your product to a new generation of eager, sophisticated college students hungry for knowledge. Their parents, and maybe even the students themselves, are often paying top dollar to learn this information, and listening to a boring professor is not high on their list of objectives. A dull, talking-head presentation will put them to sleep and have everyone question your expertise. How were your materials? Did you use visuals? Did you include participation from the class? Did you allow time for questions?

You have a limited time format in a college class, just as you will have in the business world. In fact, you probably will have to make your presentations shorter and more powerful in your real-world position, because no one wants to stay away from their own work any longer than they have to (unless you go to conferences in warm, seductive places like Hawaii, when no one will show up in the conference center anyway, because they are snorkeling, snoozing on the beach, or soaking up mai tais).

Confidence is the key to this arena, and we hope you have bunches of it by now, because if you are going to be successful in the business world, you will want to disprove the theory that public speaking is the number one fear of most adults. If you are shaky in this area, do your preplanning carefully: You must know the audience, be aware of the exact time limits, and then pace your material accordingly. If someone misunderstands your message, you need to recognize the question and be ready to clarify and expand the point in a basic language. Try to anticipate the "zaps," the unexpected questions that pop up midlecture or at the end, questions you simply cannot answer at that moment. A sharp university audience builds confidence, but a bored audience will shake your confidence if students arrive late, fall asleep, slip out early, or stop showing up at all. That is their decision, but if this happens to you, some better planning in materials and presentation style should be considered.

Find out the size, approximate ages, gender, and ethnic makeup of your potential audience and have the purpose of your presentation clearly thought out. In the business world, you are not preparing people for an undergraduate exam, in which the quickly acquired information may fade fast, like a Polaroid picture exposed to the sunshine. You are offering coworkers or superiors a full-color, full-sized permanent memory that includes any number of options: to expand their talents, improve job performance, try something new to make more money, better understand a new product, add excitement to their job, learn a new skill, or build on current skills—any number of positive reasons. If they are sitting in front of you by choice, your chances of success are vastly improved if, of course, you exude confidence, are well prepared, and—most important—know your subject.

If you think you will be asked to make presentations of any kind, you may want to consider brushing up on your public speaking skills by joining one of your local Toastmasters organizations or working with a private speech coach. Public speaking is a skill that can use periodic polishing; you will enjoy the experiences more, and your audiences will thank you.

Handling Pressure Situations

Remember the day you were teaching a freshman 101 class in your major and were asked a question you had not previously considered? Obviously, you are not about to admit that you came to class unprepared. How did you handle the situation? What did you do after class? Remember the saying that the college graduates know everything, master's graduates realize they don't know everything in a particular area of expertise, and doctoral graduates are convinced they know nothing? (Do you suppose this also implies college grads are gutsier in pressure situations than doctoral grads?)

Teaching presents a perfect opportunity for someone to ask a relevant question on which you may be fuzzy or that stumps you speechless. You have some choices here: Either come up with a solid answer, wing it, or, the best scenario, say with a confident smile, "I'll get back to you on that one." With hundreds of eyes waiting breathlessly for your reaction, you had better pull off a professional response. This quick-thinking, pressure-driven situation can happen frequently in the real world, but you can handle it. As one young man groaned after giving a particularly tense seminar to his superiors, "My Ph.D. degree now has a flexible definition. Sometimes it stands for Providing High Drama, today it was Preventing Horrendous Damage."

Interview Skills

You have had many opportunities to develop your interview skills, although the value of this practice may remain hazy. You had to prove your ability to conquer graduate school and speak with professors in your intended field of expertise. There were positions open to you as doctoral students that required additional opportunities, such as interviewing for fellowships, teaching openings, outside employment, or internships.

If you had the additional opportunity to conduct interviews for your dissertation, as many do in qualitative studies, you had a powerful position of influence. In fact, you were likely to work both sides of the interviewing process. Talk about people skills! You probably had these skills before you started, or you would not have been drawn to an interactive research study. And you know the process well. When you conducted the interview, you asked the correct questions to obtain your data; when you begin to seek a position, you will answer questions to influence your interviewer so you are chosen for the desired position.

Being tuned-in to people's reactions and being able to listen to and evaluate their responses are important skills no matter which side of the desk you sit on. The more you practice and use this skill, the better you will be at getting what you want, be it information or a job.

Intuitive Skills

We remember scanning essay questions, hoping for a question we felt sure would be on the exam, and then opening the blue book to begin spilling out creative and extensive answers. What a wonderful feeling to guess a question that appeared on the final exam! Even if the professor had repeated the material in class, giving every signal that the point was important and should be thoroughly considered, we still felt like we had just added clairvoyance to our ever-stretching skills portrait.

Some people claim intuition is nothing more than a tiny internal computer guiding our thinking and responses, sort of a subconscious technology wizard tapping into our brain cells to say, "No, don't write that, write this instead." In general, men tend not to trust this inside voice, mainly because they have trouble trusting something that does not follow a logical, play-by-their-rules style. Internal, opinionated voices do not fit in their rule books, and logic tends to rule for many analytically minded males (and, yes, some women also). Other folks, sometimes men, but far more frequently women, find this voice vibrates at all the right times, sending significant signals that are always accurate. This may be why intuition is often referred to as "women's intuition," not because women are the only ones possessing this talent, because surely all people have some talents here, but because women are the ones most likely to trust it.

Our suggestion? If you have the gift of intuition, use it, enjoy it, trust it, keep it in your bag of tricks. Listen to that voice when dealing with people and with challenging situations, when managing data, and when planning, dreaming, and resolving problems. If you do not have intuition, or do not think you have it, we beg to differ: It is there, but it is a voice that needs to be heeded. Practice. As one man said, "My partner is incredibly intuitive, she knows what's on exams, she knows which job interview will be successful, she even knows who will be on the phone when it rings." He probably could be just as successful with a little practice and a lot of willingness to trust the process. Believe in it. We do not have to know how the inside of a camera works to take startlingly clear pictures.

Listening Skills

Listening is a vital skill for employees, prospective employees, and employers at every level. Responses to questionnaires of senior executives in many different studies report that fully 80% claim the most important skill of employees is to be good listeners. Next on almost every list is for the employees to interact well with others, third is to solve problems effectively, and the fourth requirement is to understand the technology involved in their position. These skills, in this order, are coincidentally the ones executives find most lacking in the workforce. Managers, especially, must be able to hear what others are saying, because they spend the majority of their day listening to staff, coworkers, and customers. At least we hope they listen more than they speak.

Social Skills

As you consider your many academic talents, add social skills to the list. Being polite, considerate, and a good listener should be part of your makeup. You finely tuned these talents sitting patiently listening to someone expound on his or her ideas that may have borne no resemblance to your research project, but you smiled and asked pertinent questions and showed patience and perseverance. You also fine-tuned these skills when listening to exciting, informative, enlightening lectures or presentations and shared enthusiastic comments with the speaker.

The same skill will help you when job seeking, as you help create a pleasant and positive atmosphere. Showing a strong comfort level, with optimism and enthusiasm, will get you a lot further than demonstrating a grumpy, entitlement-minded personality. Call them whatever you wish—people skills, social skills, interactive skills, or simply getting-along skills—you'll need them if you intend to work and live with others.

Back to the Basics

There is a classic definition of skills assessment that is used in career counseling, applied to those with the most basic education level up to adult, graduate, and professional levels. We add these here as an overview, a quick review, and a reminder that we do have exceptional talents in at least one area, although we suspect that the process of surviving a doctoral program may allow you to claim superb talents in all three areas. Understanding this may help you pinpoint just where you would like to apply your talents. You may think this is tired, old information and start to moan, "Shoot, I know all that

SKILLS ASSESSMENT

Data (Mental)	People (Interpersonal)	Things (Physical)
Synthesizing	Mentoring	Setting up
Coordinating	Negotiating	Precision working
Analyzing	Instructing	Driving/operating
Compiling, computing	Supervising	Manipulating
Copying	Persuading	Tending
Comparing	Speaking	Feeding
	Serving, helping	Handling

stuff, why should I do it again?" but we always can use a review—and we may discover that we have sharpened skills (through our doctoral journeys) in all three traditional areas of work, which makes us even more salable on the job market.

One of the reasons you want to be clear on these processes is that, in interviews, you most likely will be asked to describe your skills and give examples of how you would offer problem-solving solutions. You might as well have some nifty expressions to toss out.

While we are playing in traditional areas, here is a quick questionnaire helping you figure out which area your brain cells and personality love the most.

Data/Mental Skills

1. Are you as thrilled as a piglet in mud when given a 3-foot list of lost research dates and asked to account for every one by the end of the day, or would you rather toss the list in the round file and go out for a round of golf? (In which case, of course, if you were in the real world, you would probably pick up your pink slip when you returned the next day.)

2. Do you shamelessly beg for the opportunity to balance the company books, figuring numbers make a lot more sense than most people you know?

3. Do you love making out budgets, compiling statistics, analyzing short- and long-term gains and losses? You probably did a lot of this budgeting to figure out how to pay for your education, and you may have juggled numbers in a quantitative dissertation, but how much did you enjoy this process?

4. Did you love roaming the library, gathering lists of obtuse facts and sorting them into logical presentations? Did you then look forward to talking about (or selling, or convincing) this material to others, or are you the sort who breaks out into hives at the thought of having to make the actual presentation? (Now we are sliding into Interpersonal Skills—more on that later.)

5. Do you find yourself choosing to balance your checkbook, check stock market quotes, or memorize the latest baseball batting averages rather than curl up in an easy chair at home with an adventure-laden book or a no-brainer television sitcom?

6. What do the words *organizing, analyzing, classifying, prioritizing, planning,* and *systematizing* do for you—make you rub your hands with glee or shiver with dread? If you are gleeful, you had better think seriously about searching for a position that allows you to use this talent. Those words can be applied to a wide range of job descriptions, so they are good to have hovering in the front of your brain.

People/Interpersonal Skills

1. Do you like working with many people around and feel energized by them? Were you one to drag books out of the stacks to read in a common room just because you needed some life around you?

2. Can you handle interruptions with ease and enjoyment, and do you tend to search out the most lighthearted of your coworkers or fellow students for a moment of mental restoration?

3. Is your favorite part of the day the lunch break, when you can hang out and talk to others to see how their work (or classes, research, projects, lives, kids, or whatever) are doing?

4. Are you the one everyone else turns to when there's a conflict or problem, because they know you can help resolve it amicably?

5. Were you the one in grad school who knew everyone's name, family members, names of cats, dogs, and kids, food preferences, and who always volunteered to write the department newsletter? And—this one is a dead giveaway on personalities—were you the one who even volunteered to organize and orchestrate the 3-day graduate student/faculty retreat to the mountains?

Things/Physical Skills

1. Can you work on a mind-numbing computer project in a windowless cubicle all day long without going nuts? (The people-preferred bias of one of the authors is showing.)

2. Do you tend to put in endless hours on trivial pursuits, sputtering around the edges of the real project until faced with an immediate deadline—as in every term paper you ever wrote? (This may fall under the category of the personality trait known as "procrastination," probably not a talent to offer freely in an official interview.)

3. Do you prefer to manipulate machinery, tinker with computers, set up special project materials, work with widgets and wonkas, or design time-saving devices in the workplace?

4. Are you one of the "kinesthetic" learners who need to touch, draw, write, or handle paper, jiggle car keys, even chew on your fingernails to learn, enjoy, or complete your work? One easy giveaway is if you tend to make lists, then create additional lists of the first list, and grin with glee when you can cross each completed item off with a firm black line to prove to yourself the chore is completed. (This is a personality trait fondly referred to as "obsessive-compulsive"—doctoral graduates probably have a pretty good dose of this talent as well.)

5. Did you resort to driving a cab or acting as a tour guide to help defray educational costs? You probably know every street and business in

your city. We hope that you also became aware of the location of different businesses that you will find quite helpful as you research the location of your future company interviews.

6. Many graduate students worked in the restaurant business to help finance tuition and are adept at juggling the physical properties as well as an occasional cranky customer. If you worked in the kitchens as a chef, as one of our friends is currently doing, you are even more adept at slinging pans, creating tempting dishes, and keeping up with a demanding, fast-paced environment. You may never want to set foot in a kitchen again, but you surely take those creative, quick-thinking, fast-reacting skills with you.

Your self-portrait as a talented, successful, clear-thinking, goal-oriented individual is almost finished, lacking a few tiny details that we leave to you to add. Personal areas such as motivation; financial and emotional goals; confidence; desire for fame, fortune, or simply a fun time; and shadowed areas are outside our lens capacity. All of these details, and more, may be camouflaged in your own photograph, but we suggest you examine them carefully. It is always smart to have some well-thought-out or clever answers available, because you will be asked questions regarding these details in many personal and professional environments. Being able to give a concise, clear, full-color illustration of who you are is a talent that will never fade.

Now is the time to consider and identify your skills. To help you get started in an organized manner, consider the following:

1. List all the positions you held during your graduate experience, such as teaching aide in History 101. Don't be shy. Consider every position now. Remember your college applications? Do not decide what is too inconsequential until you have all possible information in front of you. Do not overlook other positions. Perhaps you worked in the dean's office. That experience could contribute to additional people skills. Perhaps you headed up a university committee. Working with faculty from different departments in the university usually offers interesting opportunities. Consider all opportunities, because working with small groups can be very different from being a team leader for large groups.

2. Identify the duties for each position, such as the ordering of books, writing of syllabi, lecturing 20 hours, answering relevant questions

for 10 hours, ignoring irrelevant questions for 5 hours, and grading 100 midterm and 95 final exams. Think about all the other obligations that came with the duties. Did you have office hours? How many students did you meet with on an individual basis? What were your other responsibilities?

3. Also identify other skills required, such as research skills, writing skills, the unique speaking ability to hold the attention of 100 students, understanding different points of view, addressing the concerns of any and all students, and counseling skills.

When all this information is analyzed, you can see a pattern. The important functions are easier to identify. The lesser responsibilities can now be de-emphasized but never ignored. Clarification of your skills will enhance your ability to find an appropriate position that melds with your interests, abilities, and goals. The next two chapters help fill in the colors and shadings of your self-portrait.

CHAPTER 2

Taking a Closer Look—
Personality Profiles

Filling in the Fuzzy Parts

There are always hidden portions of our personalities that we have been too busy to showcase during our lengthy pursuit of graduate degrees. This is a good time to bring them out of the darkroom and into bright sunshine, because a complete picture is what you need to understand and be able to present on your résumé, in your interviews, in salary negotiations, and in making critical career decisions.

Two of the most popular and widely used tests are covered here. If your doctorate is in psychology, we advise you to skip right on to the next chapter because you have been living with this material for some time. We feel that these tests are simply another method of helping you to understand yourself as you prepare to enter the "real world." We would like you to understand and appreciate the way you work, your attitudes, the way you make decisions, and the lifestyle you pursue. When you become interested in learning more about your personality, you develop additional skills for understanding your behavior as well as the behavior of others.

There is greater emphasis on finding satisfying jobs when you understand what you need. Considering the many years you have spent working on your doctoral degree, you may feel that you ought to be a professor at some prestigious university, and that was your long cherished dream. It is common, however, for today's students to be forced to leave universities for the real world, and now is a good time to find your ideal new career position. Self-assessment is an excellent place to begin. When you have a clear picture of yourself, you are better prepared to market yourself by effectively presenting your abilities, interests, and skills.

Myers-Briggs Type Indicator

The Myers-Briggs Type Indicator (MBTI; Briggs & Myers, 1985) was developed by Katharine Briggs and her daughter Isabel Briggs Myers and has become one of the most widely respected and used measures of personality in organizations of every size. They based their premise of personality types on Carl Jung's theory of personality, and the resulting MBTI offers extensive descriptions of 16 distinct personality types. Although the test instrument had its beginnings in the 1940s, the MBTI has been refined over the years, and research continues today. The MBTI focuses on recognizing specific personality differences and discussions on learning to cope constructively with differences and has proven to be worthwhile and a valid instrument. There are 126 questions that address your attitudes, activities, preferred words, and perception of yourself.

Although there are 16 personality types, there are four major categories into which everyone falls. These are *extraversion* versus *introversion, sensing* versus *intuition, thinking* versus *feeling,* and *judging* versus *perceiving.* When one characteristic is selected in each category, there are 16 types of possible personalities. The types are known by initials, such as ISTJ (Introverted, Sensing, Thinking, Judging) or ENFP (Extraverted, Intuitive, Feeling, Perceiving). Some types are more common than others. There is no one occupation for each type of personality, but there are professions that seem to draw particular personality types to them like a moth to light. For instance, most research scientists share two sections of the four in personality—intuitive and thinking.

Just because there are 16 different personality types, do not think that there are only 16 personalities. Obviously, we are all unique, but each type shares many common characteristics. We all have strengths and weaknesses. The type of person we are on the MBTI, or on any other personality instrument, does not correlate with intelligence or success. There are no bad types, no good types, only characteristics that make us more open to certain work situations and occupations. We will have greater advantage of success when we are working in a profession that piques our interest and honors our inherent beliefs. Workplace environment also plays an important part of success. When we know and understand ourselves, we work in situations in which we are happiest, and the likelihood of success should increase.

Introverts/Extroverts

The first insight from the MBTI is recognizing whether we are an introvert or an extrovert. Most of us do not need a test to tell us this; we already know if we are extroverted "people-thing" oriented, doing our best work externally and action oriented, or more introverted, doing our best work inside with reflection. But knowing this explains how we interact with the world.

Introverts are often quiet, but they may or may not be shy. They are energized by quiet time as they collect their thoughts. Writers are often introverts because they thrive by themselves, delving into the ideas and structure of their written work; other writers are outgoing and ebullient, seeking fresh ideas from the outer world.

Introverts must be aware that their interest in focusing on their work and not on their relationships with others can be detrimental to the work progress. Developing relationships with coworkers can be essential in any job. Extroverts may go the other way, focusing on people instead of the necessary work—especially if the work is not challenging. Knowing and understanding our natural tendencies can lead us to emphasize and work on our less-developed side.

Introverts can become more comfortable with others by concentrating on being aware of strengths and considering opportunities for interaction. Extroverts—who are estimated to be 75% of the population (and are said to have fueled the rise in fast-food restaurants that they visit while reading McNewspapers)—are energized by being with others and crave stimulating company. They tend to like being in the middle of things, even the main attraction, but you would seldom if ever find an introvert striving for center stage.

Extroverts tend to think out loud, be better talkers than listeners, and be filled with enthusiasm for new projects and adventures. Their introverted counterparts can be found on the edges of the action, thinking things through carefully before acting, and may hesitate before speaking their minds unless urged to contribute.

This is the bottom line: Introverts and extroverts are different, not better or worse than the other, just different. Having both in a work environment adds richness, fun, productivity, and plenty of silly jokes.

Sensing/Intuition

The second category of the MBTI concerns the way we attain information, the way we naturally learn. Sensing is one category; intuition is the other. People sharing the sensing mode usually consider the present, how knowledge affects the here and now. People who use intuition to gather information are typically more future-oriented, trying to determine how particular data may affect future endeavors.

Thinking/Feeling

The third area to discover is the method we use to make decisions. Do we decide by thinking or feeling? Some of us sense how we are going to react, how we think, and what we should do. Decisions often are made according to one's values. This type of decision-making process is considered a subjective approach. Others carefully weigh each decision, considering all sides of the issue, and then come to a conclusion using logic—or at least they think they are logical. This mode of making decisions is considered an objective approach. Professors more often fall into this category; students wander all over the map but may be taught that the objective method is best. (They may not be comfortable with it but go along because they think it is the only acceptable method.)

Perceiving/Judging

The last area of the MBTI addresses our preferred mode for living. Do we enjoy planning each day in advance so that our time is wisely used? Or do we love spontaneity and take advantage of last-minute opportunities, adventures, and parties? The two areas of this category are judging and perceiving. Judging does not mean judgmental but describes one who prefers to have plans, be organized, and seek closure. (One friend of ours claims that her "J" score is so high that she plans her work wardrobe two weeks in advance. Some of us cannot even relate to the concept, much less put it in action.)

Perceiving refers to a more open-ended lifestyle, in which decisions may be last minute—they may change their clothes four times before they dash out the door for work. Obviously, there are ramifications to the two types of behavior. You may miss out on opportunities because you drive your friends away due to your inability to commit early to plans. On the other hand, circumstances change, and, if you decide at the last minute, other interesting possibilities may appear. New opportunities are taken advantage of because you are not locked into obligations and plans.

We would not dream of suggesting that anyone try to change their basic personality, but all of us can improve our skills in understanding our own style of interaction as well as the traits of others.

The MBTI is an excellent inventory for individuals to analyze their interests, their preferred method of communication style, their values, and their skills. Even though we fall into one basic type, there are overlaps into similar personality styles, and different circumstances may push us into pursuing nonpreferred responses. And we do use all characteristics of other types some of the time. The MBTI tells us where we naturally head, but it does not mean we are limited to any one method of working and acting. It is just that we are comfortable heading in one direction, and, if we decide we want to work in another method, we must make a conscious effort to go that direction.

We suggest you take the MBTI, for fun, for learning, for curiosity, or for interesting interview language, if nothing else. If you do not have access to a university or private career office, explore any state or community colleges near you. Many allow residents to take a test (it may cost a few dollars), meet with a counselor, and discuss the results.

Strong Interest Inventory

The Strong Interest Inventory (Strong, 1985) is a commonly administered test at any university, college, and career service organization. The Strong was first published in 1927 and has undergone several revisions. It is considered to be one of the most reliable tests of its kind, and students attending such universities as Stanford are encouraged to use the results when researching jobs. Validity of this inventory is strong.

This test is unlike the MBTI in that it is concerned with careers, not focused on personality. There are 325 multiple-choice questions assessing your interests in specific types of work and your individual characteristics; 6 concern general occupational themes, 23 are basic interest scales, and the other 207 questions are occupational scales. The Strong is a measure of interests, not abilities. However, when we like to do something, we are likely to be good at it. The answers you give are matched with other people in particular careers. Studies have shown that people in any given career are likely to share many interests. These interests include school subjects and other activities relating to that career. Risk takers probably will not be as happy as pigs in mud, for example, if they end up wallowing in a career slot that is repetitive, is mundane, and requires no creativity or change of pace.

The Strong matches a person's interest and shows similarities with John Holland's six general occupational themes (Holland, 1997; for a terrific test and analysis of Holland's six types, go to self-directed-search.com). These include Realistic, Artistic, Investigative, Social, Enterprising, and Conventional. These groups are selected to cover a vast selection of occupations. Although any one individual does not fall neatly into one category, a counselor will examine in which group you score the highest number of responses. Also considered is the number of responses in the other categories.

All your answers are analyzed and matched with people already in the workforce. Those people who are happy and successful with their careers have specific characteristics that are matched with your interests. In other words, your responses to the questions on the test likely would match those people in a particular career, and, consequently, you would be more likely to be happy if you share the same type of work.

This is not to say that you can only be happy with one career. The results show your strongest areas of interest. There are many possibilities for everyone. If you are interested in the Strong, find a qualified person to administer the test and to evaluate the results. Unless you have a doctorate in the psychological area, you may have trouble understanding and fully using the results.

As with any test taking in the areas of career counseling, no one is limited to only one career option. The MBTI and the Strong have a long and successful history, with positive language offering pertinent information for you as an individual and in your choice of career. Thus, they both should be considered. The more options we consider, the better decisions we will make regarding our work lives.

You do not need to change who you are, but we are assuming you wish to better understand who you are and where you would like to be for an exciting career. Knowing and understanding natural tendencies will help us better understand ourselves as well as people we meet.

Before we launch further into this story, we'll share a common game played by career counselors and outplacement specialists for clients with varied educational levels. A list of 132 buzzwords follows (you are free to add to this list, of course), and you will find that many of these words are woven into your personality. Depending on the situation, you may be able to relate to most of them. Instead of claiming them all as inherent traits that you have had since birth, however, and instead of trying to include a massive list on a résumé or announcing them breathlessly in an interview, we suggest you follow a common path:

Read them over slowly.

Check all the traits you feel you have at any given time.

Choose about 12 that you feel are your strongest selling points.

Recognize that you may choose different words for different job applications, depending on the position you are seeking, but for now 12 is a good starting place.

Now narrow the list to six attributes.

(Depending on your bravery level, offer a copy of this list to several good friends and ask them to identify six to eight attributes they feel you possess in abundance. Think twice about family member input—they may dream up some creative attributes that would not be the slightest bit helpful in your employment search.)

So, now you have a specialized list of personality quirks, and you have a good idea how to use them best as well as how to be flexible and pull out the best traits to fit the situation. You also know that many highly qualified folks share your specialized list, but each attribute will appear different because it belongs to a different person. Your DNA, culture, family, community, education, and a zillion other influences are combining to make you a one-of-a-kind individual—but one with a doctorate.

Now that your brain is working in a list mode, we give it one more set of words that will help you in analyzing your abilities and interests. These are active verbs, always handy to have on the tip of your tongue or when building a résumé or a career.

PERSONAL/SELF-MANAGEMENT

Accurate	Focused	Poised
Active	Frank	Polite
Adaptable	Friendly	Positive
Adventurous	Generous	Precise
Affectionate	Genuine	Progressive
Aggressive	Goal-oriented	Prudent
Alert	Good-natured	Purposeful
Ambitious	Healthy	Quick-thinking
Analytical	Helpful	Quiet
Assertive	Honest	Rational
Attractive	Hopeful	Realistic
Broad-minded	Humorous	Reflective
Calm	Imaginative	Relaxed
Capable	Independent	Reliable
Careful	Individualistic	Responsible
Charitable	Industrious	Secure
Charming	Intellectual	Self-confident
Clear-thinking	Introspective	Self-controlled
Clever	Intuitive	Sensible
Committed	Inventive	Serene
Competitive	Joiner	Sincere
Confident	Kind	Sociable
Conscientious	Leader	Spontaneous
Conservative	Lighthearted	Stable
Considerate	Likable	Steady
Consistent	Logical	Strong
Cooperative	Loyal	Strong-minded
Courageous	Mature	Successful
Creative	Methodical	Tactful
Curious	Meticulous	Teachable
Daring	Moderate	Tenacious
Deliberate	Modest	Thorough
Determined	Motivated	Thoughtful
Dignified	Natural	Tolerant
Discreet	Open-minded	Tough
Eager	Optimistic	Trusting
Easygoing	Organized	Trustworthy
Efficient	Original	Unassuming
Empathetic	Outgoing	Understanding
Energetic	Painstaking	Versatile
Fair-minded	Patient	Well-educated
Farsighted	Perfectionist	Wholesome
Firm	Persevering	Wise
Flexible	Pleasant	Witty

ACTIVE VERB LIST

Analyzed

Answered

Collaborated

Communicated

Conducted

Created

Disciplined

Drew inferences

Focused

Graded

Informed

Initiated

Interested

Led

Located

Managed time well

Mentored

Motivated

Offered alternative solutions

Planned

Prepared

Presented

Presented views

Read

Reduced

Researched

Showed sense of humor

Solved

Taught

Worked

Wrote

Values Check

There is one more area to examine that will come in handy not only during your job search but in all further decisions about your working life. This is a thoughtful look at your value system. Each of us has our own values and value system, and it is tied closely with our ethics. We are assuming you had ethics courses in your program and have entered into—or been dragged into—deep discussions about ethical issues, so you probably have a good idea where you stand about these matters. But we still would like to encourage you to think about future goals. Have you considered your ideal lifestyle, the type of people you want to be around, the culture of your workplace, the extent you want to be in control of your work, and how high you would like to travel in an organization?

What are your core beliefs, your character, your philosophy of life? How do you live by your ethical standards, choose your friendships, make decisions about what is right and wrong? What are your material needs, do you care what part of the country spells "h-o-m-e," and would you move anywhere if the salary (or other perks) enticed you? Are you willing to work 70 hours a week? Is security, position, advancement, or prestige important? Is being a leader on your goal list? Even political beliefs may be relied on, or challenged, in certain positions.

Now that we have boggled your brain, we'll offer two miniversions of values profiles, neither of them the slightest bit scientific, but it is time to lighten up and have some fun. There are other value instruments, of course, the solid, statistically based tests you can find at your career center or from a career counselor. For now, lighten up:

Imagine there are five events going on simultaneously that need to be addressed:

1. The telephone is ringing.

2. The kids are screaming.

3. Someone is yelling and banging on the front door.

4. Your laundry is hanging outside, and rain is coming down.

5. The kitchen water faucet is running.

In what order would you take care of these problems? Jot down your answers in order, then look at the explanation after you have made your decision. The following numbers represent something in your life that is important to you:

1. The phone = your job or career.

2. The kids = your family.

3. The visitor = your friends.

4. The laundry = your sex life.

5. The running water = money or wealth.

How close does this test match your priorities in life?

Here is one more value evaluation, this one a little bit more serious in honor of those who thought they were buying a serious book.

Rank the following priorities in order from 1 to 6, 1 being top priority, 6 being least important to you at this stage in your life. (We listed them in alphabetical order, so don't let the presentation color your thinking.) There are many other values, of course, and you are free to make up your own list, but this is a start.

1. Challenge

2. Family

3. Financial security

4. Independence

5. Power

6. Service to others

Take another look at your top two or three choices, and then ask yourself as you research career opportunities: Does this position offer the values that are most important to me? If not, point your camera in another direction and focus on another company that is compatible with your goals.

We keep referring to the topic of values because we feel it is a critical component to finding "institutional fit" in your future, and we hope your values will continue to ripple through your thinking processes throughout your adult life. You will find reminders of your value system reappearing near the end of Chapter 4 (Applying Your Skills to the Job Market), in Chapter 8 (Networking), and in Chapter 10 (Perfecting Interview Skills).

If you are interested, there are many other instruments that you can play with for a values review. This brief sample is here to give you an idea of what is available. These tests are not as widely used as the personality tests, but they are still beneficial. As you continue to review your most selling traits, we encourage you also to keep in mind the values that are most important to you.

Now that you have a wide-eyed picture of your multiple transferable skills from Chapter 1 and can speak volumes about your delightful personality quirks and quarks, and now that you understand your innate ability to work in almost any challenging environment, we would like to expand your portrait to include your skills with others, known popularly as "people skills"—influences on those around you. You can decide whether your people skills are terrific or whether they need to be addressed a little more clearly, and Chapter 3 should help you focus on this all-important talent.

References

Briggs, Katharine C., & Myers, Isabel Briggs. (1988). *Myers-Briggs Type Indicator.* Palo Alto, CA: Consulting Psychologists Press.

Holland, J. L. (1997). *Making vocational choices: A theory of vocational personalities and work environments.* Odessa, FL: Psychological Assessment Resources, Inc.

Strong, Edward K., Jr. (1985). *Strong Interest Inventory.* Palo Alto, CA: Stanford University Press.

CHAPTER 3

Identifying Interactive Skills

What's Mine Is Mine, and What's Yours May Be Mine, Too.

One of the most difficult assignments we have in plotting strategies for launching a successful career is figuring out how to differentiate our own personality traits and talents from the hordes of other applicants. This is the one challenge you probably have encountered since your college application, followed by similar challenges while filling out forms for graduate school, then again for a doctoral program. We ought to have figured out by now how unique we are, wouldn't you think? But many of us have been too busy to spend time analyzing ourselves.

Let's push out your zoom lens just a bit, keeping yourself in sharp focus but opening the lens to bring in the aspects of your personality that you use to interact with others. People tell us they often were so immersed in their own research and writing that they were likely to answer with a fuzzy "Who, me?" when asked to describe themselves. Perhaps the only current mental images are from your immediate past, as a determined student, bone-weary library patron, compulsive rewriter, or an accomplished but bleary-eyed all-nighter computer wizard, with lousy nutritional habits and a tendency to talk about minute details on page 203 of your dissertation.

All of this fuzzy focus will pass—or, with luck, already has passed—and now you are ready to add some sharp details to your growing self-portrait.

This is an important exercise, because up to now you have received little or no support or training to achieve top jobs outside academia. And, just as in your classes, you will encounter as many diverse personalities and cultural backgrounds as you can imagine. Your talents must mesh productively with others in the workplace.

Let's take a look at the big picture to see what areas you feel would best fit your personality and goals. Many areas of influence most likely will be combined into one position; rarely, if ever, do you work alone or in a vacuum with no outside challenges or influences, even in start-up, upstart Internet companies. Let's look at the picture of what is considered when you work and interact with others who have quite different talents. The general areas of skills and behaviors that are considered and evaluated by employers (depending on the industry, of course) are communication, leadership, being a team player, teaching, motivating, training, mentoring, getting along with others, empowering others, taking instruction, interpreting others' ideas, and marketing yourself.

Communication

Communication is the foundation of all human interaction and is an ability highly prized in every environment, from school to work, and in every community. It is how people solve problems, reach consensus, build relationships, and solve conflicts. We would like to think you are a terrific communicator by now; after all, you spent years defending your positions, explaining your thinking processes, and re-forming your opinions in doctoral work. Sometimes you listened to others and changed your mind; other times you simply pointed the camera off to infinity and continued to argue your own point of view. Did you wilt under intense scrutiny or relish the chance to take on a new challenge? Different situations call for different responses, the old flexible focus game again. Just know that your resiliency will bode well for the future.

One Ph.D. graduate now working in Silicon Valley stated that his excellence in communication is the key to his present working success. As he describes a typical working day, most of what he does centers around the ability to listen to others, express his opinions smoothly and without emotional overload, and write in a clear and concise manner—all effective communication skills. He remembers classroom presentations and the doctoral defense when he had a specific time limit to convince others of his position, a talent that contributes to his current upward progress in high tech: "I knew enough about computers to survive graduate school," he said, "but didn't consider I could thrive in high tech. Turns out my communication skills were a big help; the programs are easy to pick up."

As this former student pointed out, high tech is a great field for doctoral graduates in the humanities. The arena is growing so quickly that rules are constantly changing, a refreshing change of pace from rule-bound academia. The new young companies in this industry seek people who are independent, tenacious, able to recognize and solve problems, and self-directed. They seek those who thrive on lack of structure, who can move quickly to create and/or implement new ideas, who are willing to work more than a 40-hour week in the beginning, and who can communicate their needs and expectations smoothly.

Of course, high tech is not the only arena requiring clear and concise written and verbal communication skills. Every environment—school, work, or play—depends on competent communication skills. We may decide to shorten our presentations to capture the MTV generation, slow down our conversations in group discussions, or race through boring material to get to the juicy parts, but interacting with others will always be the name of this game.

Leadership

Consider the skills you used to identify a goal or a vision. What activities did you plan or pursue to involve others in your cause? When did you work together with a group for a common purpose?

A leader must identify a problem, understand the process to change, engage others to transform, and build teams able to work for a common goal. Highly educated people work with ideas, are interested in solutions, and recognize the potential power of problem solving. Productive leaders typically have powerful interactive skills as they resolve thorny issues and pursue mutually beneficial goals.

A vision for many growing businesses includes shared leadership, team efforts, mutual goal-setting, and progressive growth. People with leadership strengths are sought after and compensated well. If you expect to come out of a doctoral program and be offered the position of CEO of General Motors, however, you need a reality check. That is not to say you don't have the ability—we have met many folks with doctorates who have more common sense, morals, mental agility, and reasonable goal-reaching talents than most of the popular names being flashed on national news programs. But both academia and business seem to think a little training might be necessary before becoming top banana, and rightly so.

Unless, of course, you jump onto the entrepreneurial bandwagon and follow the Texas cowgirl who came out of school with a doctorate in psychology and promptly started her own investment management firm. "A business manager, an assistant, and a lot of gumption were the first requirements," she reported. "And patience," she added a few minutes later in her soft Texas drawl. "I work with every education level and cultural background and use every skill I perfected in graduate school with my staff: sweet talkin', cajolin', nudgin', beggin', promisin' promotions, and I'm even considerin' bribery. Whatever works, honey." We think she may rewrite the books on both entrepreneurial styles and leadership before she's through.

Not everyone wants to be in the top spot; indeed, we have read about quite a few women (and even a very few men) who, upon reaching the top corner office, promptly restructure the company from a hierarchical structure into a "humanist" style, in which communication between all levels is available and encouraged. Why? "Because it's lonely up there," several women have reported with a smile. To them, leadership is a group effort, not a solitary spot.

Others—mostly men but increasingly women—are so good at climbing ladders and trampling competitors that they do not consider counting the broken bodies in their mad scramble to the top. These warriors are much in evidence today, in spite of the current writings and requests to share talents in leadership positions. As one fellow defended his dramatic climb, "Truman said it best, 'The buck stops here.' Someone has to be willing to take the final responsibility." Absolutely true, but it is also wise to know where you feel most comfortable. If taking full responsibility does not give you a thrill or makes you shiver in dread right down to your toenails, then look for a company with shared leadership roles in which you have a chance to continue learning and growing.

Team Player

Are you a good team player? Can you work well with others without dictating, stepping on toes, or ignoring the ideas and concepts of your fellow workers? People with advanced degrees are notorious for being good at working alone. After all, you were forced to take exams and write papers and the dissertation by yourself, no matter how hard you may have thought about attempting to bribe a clever colleague to help you.

But how good are you at working with others? Consider the times you were forced to make a presentation with a group. You may not have been appreciative of having to work with some of the students. You may have resented the time you were forced to contribute more time than the others because the quality of their work was not up to your standards. However, the experience of the group project gave you the opportunity to interact. You worked for a common goal. And obviously you survived, relatively intact.

Teams continue to be an important aspect of today's workplace. Your ability to understand different points of view, different positions, and different pieces of the puzzle will only help you to work for a larger organization that prefers team spirit and the ability to work toward a shared goal. Working in teams is becoming more prevalent in many businesses, so you might want to tout this skill.

Teaching

Most of us in doctoral programs spent many hours teaching, either on a regular basis or contributing to classroom teaching by presenting part-time. The preparation includes interacting positively with eager students, taking on the challenge of turning a reluctant class into an energetic group of cooperative and curious scholars, creating and maintaining a positive learning environment, and writing and grading exams.

Preparing for each class is a time-consuming project, unless you are the type to stand and deliver the identical information in the same monotone and ponderous pitch year after boring year. Today, whatever your delivery style, standing in front of the students and lecturing is only one of the requirements to being viewed as a top-notch instructor. You probably spent many hours considering the course work to be covered, weeding out old information, and researching and gathering new plums to pass on. You probably spent an equal amount of time covering your style and method of presentation as well as remaining up-to-date on visual and audio aids.

The class delivery time is especially valuable because if you have the ability to entertain and hold the attention of hundreds of students who have other interests, you certainly can hold the attention of executives and other workers who want to hear you speak. And you undoubtedly have been asked to conduct a seminar for reluctant or recalcitrant folks who would rather file their fingernails or hide under their desks than sit through another required instruction session. No matter what field you go into, you will find that you will be instructing, teaching, and selling ideas or products or solutions to others. Take these opportunities whenever possible, and if you get a few discouraging evaluations, so what? You can't please all the folks all the time. And you will probably take home a healthy paycheck, which always softens other minor disappointments.

Motivating

How did you encourage others or keep your own head above water? How did you finish all the required reading, papers, presentations, and proper preparation for exams?

Students often form study groups during their doctoral years, mainly because it is obvious that with so much material covered during the quarter or semester, one would be hard pressed to feel like an expert in all areas of course work. Forming groups, dividing the work, and leading a discussion cut down the time enormously.

All the encouragement to help your fellow students through the hard times and pressing others to perform well so that you too would look good paid off when grades were distributed. All the time spent motivating your fellow classmates to finish their dissertations (as they pushed you to do the same) so you could share that joyous graduation date is now appreciated.

And how about all the students in your classes? Obviously, some of the material you had to teach may not have contained the most interesting or irresistible bits of information. Yet, you tried to present the facts in a fascinating manner, because you wanted your students to share your understanding about the subject. Even student evaluations held the power to encourage or discourage you.

So how do you motivate others? Money is often considered the biggest motivator of all, but it is not in abundant supply in academia at any level. Rewards in universities for students are primarily in grades; for professors, promotions, tenure, and recognition by publication are all satisfactory rewards. But in business? Ahhh, that is where dollar bills often have unvarnished power to motivate. Other aspects—job satisfaction, potential for advancement, continued learning, even compliments—are motivators also, but decent salary has the power to motivate—and also to frustrate, mandate, or eliminate, but we won't go into that. It's enough to have you know how to figure out what is the lure that motivates you as well as others with whom you work. Some may even work just for a pat on the back or a sincere compliment. But maybe they don't have the same need to eat that we do?

Training

You may have worn many hats during your academic travels, most likely including instructor, teacher, teaching assistant, presenter, panelist, moderator, instigator, peacemaker, group contributor, and class leader.

But did you ever think of yourself as a trainer? Because you are, or can be, in the blink of an eye, and you will use all these talents with ease. Anyone who has ever stood in front of a group to present material in any form, shape, or length can be called a trainer. Every time you stood in front of students or colleagues to exchange ideas and share information, you were training. Every time you inspired others to laugh, to accept a difficult change, or to reach out for a new idea, you were conducting valuable training sessions.

The beauty of this is that trainers are a hot commodity in the current business world, and they are in high demand for a multitude of teaching/ training areas. Pick any business, from manufacturing to consulting to counseling to nonprofit to health care to any other specialty, and strong trainers will be valuable employees. You may train new employees in company policy, update current employees in procedures, teach new skills from computers to communication, help others develop additional skills in techniques or talents, educate employees in highly charged areas ranging from sexual harassment to discrimination lawsuits, or simply be on site (with a fancy office, of course) to deal with whatever issues come up.

And you don't have to have a doctorate in psychology to be a trainer, although it certainly will open more doors if you do. In fact, very often you don't even need a doctorate at all (oops, the secret is out), but there is no denying that those three initials after your name send a powerful message that yes, you can do this work wonderfully, and you will not only bring additional expertise to the training seminars but take responsibility for having the material ready and will be able to present it in understandable form. Researching and synthesizing ideas is your strong suit, remember? Let's hope presenting them is also a well-honed skill.

"But what would I train people to do?" you may be asking at this point. The easy answer: *Anything.* You may have a doctorate in the marriage customs of the natives in Machu Picchu, or be able to discuss the pros and cons of every leadership theory of the last hundred years, or know the intimate workings of a remote school district in the Appalachian mountains, or be able to spit out statistics about the speed at which pregnant rats can race through mazes, but you definitely know how to research and present your material. And unless the training you are asked to conduct is superbly technical, you can find a way to do it. If someone asked you to conduct communication seminars, or customer service requirements classes, or offer a series of basic computer programs at their place of business, of course you could! All you need is a list of what they envision as their goals, a little homework, and you're off and leading professional seminars.

Suppose someone in a human resources department asked you to conduct a 3-day workshop on writing and public speaking skills. Well, if anyone knows about this stuff, it's you! Ask what kind of writing employees are expected to do, then, if you're not sure about the public speaking rules of the day, take a quick run through a bookstore or spend a couple of hours on the Internet, and you will be buried in so much material your biggest problem will be winnowing it down to 3 days' worth. (But prepare an extra day's worth, just in case. You never know when your audience will have a zombie response level, and you get talking so fast trying to hold their interest that you cannot possibly stretch the information for the full time.)

What if you were asked to hold customer service training sessions for a new group of employees? This happened to a friend of ours, and she immediately discovered a new profession by doing her research and projecting confidence. She asked for the company's original booklet, which she then rewrote and expanded with additional research and updated information. She boldly copyrighted her material and is currently conducting extensive training sessions for hefty pay. She then expanded the concept and marketed herself to other companies. Because each company has slightly different needs, she tweaks the material to reflect their company style and hops off to another 6-week or 6-month training module. She is having a wonderful, challenging, exciting time and is laughing all the way to the bank.

"But what if I can't stand to be in front of a group, no matter how well I know the material?" you ask in trembling voice.

Then don't bother calling yourself a trainer. Maybe you ought to look into independent research positions.

Mentoring

Many graduates come away from the doctoral experience complaining that they were not mentored, that no one was around to support them. They claim that faculty have too many students and have no time to mentor. This "culture of neglect" is often felt among doctoral students. If your experience was different and someone special or several people mentored you, giving you insights into the program or the process, then you are indeed fortunate. And, hopefully, if you were one of the lucky few, as you moved through your own program, you reached out to mentor someone in the early doctoral stages.

"I was lucky," reported one recent graduate. "I met a student in her second year during the orientation process. She immediately suggested the progression of classes. We became close friends and confidantes." The mentoring that this student received reinforced her desire to help other students. The ability to mentor is important all through our lives.

Mentoring is entering a new stage today. Due to the fast-paced life in the business world, people tend to change jobs and careers more easily and far more frequently than in the past. Companies have had little success attempting to pair mentors and protégés by a deliberate process. The best way seems to be for everyone to take responsibility and set up his or her relationships. In other words, mentoring has become more informal and more dependent on each individual to take charge, build the relationships, and develop a "web on connections," which will help in all future endeavors.

Because we change jobs more rapidly now, one will have an advantage if he or she arranges for several mentors, more commonly known as the *learning network,* in which colleagues and personal contacts make connections that cross paths in many different ways. These interactions may be in structured meetings or informal gatherings. One might assume that if two people are working in competing businesses, they will not relate well to each other. However, this is not the case. "I used a friend in a competing bank as a wonderful sounding board" stated a bank president. Involving others who share the same interest will broaden your outlook of the business. You will grow and those with whom you share thoughts also will grow. When we verbalize our thoughts, we rise to the next level, just as we did in graduate school. Better understanding leads to further thought and developments.

Mentoring involves two people who both should benefit from the experience. When you have several mentors and can network successfully, you are more likely to find more opportunities. When you can suggest a person for a responsible job and that person works well, you may be rewarded when you are searching for someone with different skills. When you enter the business world, these skills will be essential to your upward mobility. And isn't mobility the whole point?

Getting Along With Others

Can you get along well with all types of personalities? If you can, you are most fortunate, because you are among the few. All of us have been in uncomfortable positions, perhaps intimidated or even terrorized by people in positions of influence, but we know we are forced to get through these times by remembering what is truly important.

How do you effectively persuade a person who has different ideas that your ideas also should be considered? How do you bring out the closed personality when you really need some information? Typically, a sense of humor—the ability to laugh and enjoy others—is a successful tool in dealing with difficult people. Be prepared to explain how you deal successfully with such people in case you are asked that question when you are in the job interview process or when you are considering going to work for a company that has many different opportunities and challenging personalities.

Remember how you used your skills to interact with others during the years in graduate school? Some might argue that universities are filled with difficult people and you made your way successfully through that experience. But it is not just academia that is so; the business world also is full of so many types of people of every level of intelligence and ambition and values that it behooves all of us to work on our "getting along" skills.

Empowering Others

Yes, it is hard to hand power over to others. It is a rare skill and commodity to be nurtured and treasured. However, in the long run, you will appreciate not having to make all the decisions and instead learn to rely on others. Remember preparing for exams and turning over sections to others for the review? Yes, it worked, it cut down on your time and certainly evened out the workload. You may not have loved the process; in fact, you might have bitten your tongue almost out of your head, but it did work. Sometimes, you even liked yourself afterward.

Besides, another point of view is valid. As we empower others, we also reinforce our own beliefs or decide that another point of view is more pertinent. Either way, we personally benefit. So empowering is not really about giving away power. What it really means is helping others, trusting others to develop and progress so that a common goal is achieved. If you have teaching experience, you know all about the excitement and reward that comes from empowering students to become independent, creative thinkers and problem solvers.

Taking Instruction

There were probably some moments when you hated being squeezed into classroom seats and forced to listen to a boring lecture. We all remember when a professor's conclusion was bizarre, yet we had to sit in our seats and consider the possibility that this highly educated individual must be right. Many times we were not persuaded by the arguments but felt forced to accept that the statements had validity; other times, admittedly, we found ourselves wanting to giggle out loud, or we let out a big "ah-ha!" when we learned a powerful new concept.

At different stages in our lives, we will most likely have to work in situations in which we will be second-guessed, in which we will not always have the last say, in which we will not always be right, in which we will get advice when we least want it. When we leave academics and move into business, we still will need to listen to those in superior positions, and, if we are smart, we also will consider ideas from people who are in less strategic positions. Get used to being told what to do, get used to keeping your listening skills in tune. We have been told by a variety of employees that having to take instruction from subordinates is a tough challenge emotionally but a vital one for completing tasks—if the subordinates know what they are talking about, of course. You have to decide which is more important, your ego or your work. Better yet, decide how to keep both buzzing along smoothly.

Interpreting Others' Ideas

Listening to others probably helped you identify your own beliefs. Remember how an idea advanced your own analogy? In business, you do not want to dismiss other ideas contrary to your own. Consider these ideas first as you develop your own plan.

Most of us know students who have worked hard to develop a new theory or a new outlook on a current problem. Some professors will stand on the sidelines and cheer enthusiastically; others are unable to leave the students' ideas alone and will fiddle with them or even claim the credit.

We all have heard stories about original ideas being published under someone else's name; this doesn't just happen among Hollywood scriptwriters. How will you use this information in the future to make sure credit is given to you? Or is that important to you? The bottom line is that letting others express themselves completely can be a rewarding and learning experience, as long as they are not stealing your thunder. (Yes, we know, it can also be a crushing bother, but that's simply part of the communication process.)

Marketing Yourself

During the academic years, many doctoral students are secure in their work because, for the moment, they know where they are going (and it's usually a dash to the next class). Typically, each of us spent a few years covering our course work and then on to the dissertation stage. We really did not have to market ourselves, we just had to stay in the lock-step process. Our work expressed what we did and how we felt, and it determined how quickly we progressed through the years of schooling.

You are changing the picture now, however, and creating a new set of goals. You must be able to market yourself if you have not already done so. You may have a difficult time bragging about your accomplishments and, of course, downplaying your weaknesses. However, if you don't feel strongly about your talents, then who will? Businesses will not typically try to convince you that you are needed in their companies—you have to convince them that they cannot function efficiently without you.

What do you offer the workplace of your choice? Think about different ways you can showcase your skills. This may be an arduous task for one who has previously had to rely primarily on snippets of ideas or wiggly concepts, but hard, dependable data are needed now—not statistical tables or discussions of null hypotheses or esoteric theories, unless you are going into research. Skills. Talents. Show what you can do.

Recognizing that your talents can be blended with the talents of others will only make you a more appreciated employee. Remember, an interviewer outside the ivory tower wants to know what you can do and how you will benefit his or her company by doing the work and being a team player in the culture. You will fit into the culture by working with others, by interacting with one another's talents. You will be a more attractive employee when you understand the company environment and are willing to work in its manner to do your very best.

So what are the primary colors in this portrait? We might capture a sky-blue hue, representing strong communication; an easy-to-live-with green for blending teaching, mentoring, and training skills; and solid yellow, a strong "mind" color, for listening, taking instruction, considering ideas of others. Then we will add a bright streak of red—an energy color—for marketing ourselves in a successful manner.

We have now completed the three chapters of a self-assessment portrait, including transferable scholarly powers, personality review, and people skills. It is time to develop this picture and examine ways to broadcast our talents into the "real world."

PART II

CHAPTER 4

Applying Your Skills to the Job Market

Roads Not Yet Taken

You have done most of your homework already—you have an accurate picture of your academic gifts and how these gifts interact with others in group/work settings. You also have filled in the fuzzy spaces of your highly developed and enchanting personality. We hope that you are now in a position to truly understand yourself and to recognize that your potential is unlimited. You are qualified to do many things other than teach in a university setting. We suggest you broaden your job search by aiming your camera at as many diverse fields as possible, be it computers, or information-oriented companies, or technical companies, or public relations or advertising, foundations, research institutions, think tanks, even energy fields (no pun intended this time), or radio/television. One woman we spoke with is editing technical journals; a young man is trying his hand at travel books. The choices are limitless.

You are aware of your organizational and technical skills, your management style, and relationship abilities. How about fields of interest? If you took the Strong Interest Inventory and the Myers-Briggs Type Indicator, you understand your interests, talents, experience, and goals.

We hope you have gone to your university career center to discuss various careers, prowled through your local bookstore for ideas and information, or tapped into up-to-the-minute information found on the Internet. This book cannot cover all potential areas of work, but it can help make your research more productive. Check for job descriptions in the ads, examine the salary ranges of different opportunities (try Internet sites of the Bureau of Labor Statistics—www.stats/bls/gov—and the *Wall Street Journal*—www. careers/wsj.com—both good places to begin salary comparison research), and then position yourself so that your abilities and interests will exceed the hiring manager's expectations.

If you found an internship in the "real world" during your time in academia, focus on the positive aspects of that experience. What did you learn from working in that setting? What did you contribute? What could be used today? Remember that knowledge is power and that knowledge does not have to be limited to what was learned in the classroom. Any journals and local newspapers also add to your knowledge of what is going on in the job market. Explore all avenues that you can.

We have an additional suggestion: If possible, go directly to your university career center. It will be run (we assume) by a talented, knowledgeable, helpful staff able to administer personality and career tests and offer job searching information. There are other services available, but the assistance offered may not be what the student is seeking. You need to be smart and selective. Two graduates, writing about the identical Ivy League university (which shall remain nameless but starts with an *H* and gets a lot of snowstorms), reported directly opposite results. One said the help she received was "Tops! Very valuable, I owe them everything!" whereas another felt that the career center was never involved in helping students get jobs:

> They kept wanting me to be in focus/discussion groups. . . . I was not comfortable with the pseudo-psychology group-therapy orientation. I wanted hard, practical advice about the corporate world—including the business aspects of getting hired and working in commercial publishing, theater, and writing corners of the world.

Some reported a great deal of individual help from their universities; others said there was barely any individualism. You need to make the system work for you.

Planning

What are your special skills? Where do YOU belong in the real world? Will you immediately become President of IBM, or will you settle for a nice, comfy job in middle management? Are you so desperate that you would be grateful for any position anywhere, just to get you off the unemployment line? A critical question here is, did you go through a doctoral program thinking that the process will determine your future direction in life?

That preconceived notion is a stumbling block for many, as Anita Rogers, Ed.D., career counselor and human resource manager, told us:

> If you're not clear when you go into a program, if you think a pro-gram is going to fix your lack of direction, [it won't]. It's going to make it worse, because it will scatter you in all kinds of directions, and you won't have the time to focus on yourself, which is what you really need to do. Then you will spend time after you have finished, recovering from burnout . . . and also trying to figure out your new direction as a new person.

She added that she has seen many instances in which graduates put intense pressure on themselves to "become something as important as the degree im-plies."

And the degree does imply importance, as seen in the words of Fred Gal-loway, doctoral graduate from Harvard, current Associate Dean of Education at the University of San Diego and former higher education association and private sector researcher:

> A doctorate sends a signal to people that you have adhesiveness . . . a stick-to-it-iveness to be able to see a big project from start to finish . . . and do it in a high-quality way. It tells people you have a certain set of skills.

We agree. We know that the degree often opens unique and interesting doors, but you must have a plan and an idea of what you would like to do. If you did not have a plan during your graduate program, you certainly had better put one together now.

Goals

Many new doctoral graduates have to restructure goals that may have been nurtured and cherished for a lifetime, as Jennifer Carrell told us:

> Since before I can remember, I have wanted to write stories. How-ever, as I grew up and faced a few basic facts about money, I found I could not expect fiction to be a paying proposition, so I chose a

career that I thought would be compatible with writing, as well as interesting, and useful. I love the treasure hunt of scholarship, I love literature and theater, and I thought of teaching as a noble profession—a chance to make a career out of doing something useful and good in the world.

So she made teaching her biggest dream.

Jennifer earned many teaching awards as an adjunct, but she was not offered a tenured position. She reported that she might consider reapplying for a tenured spot down the road, but only after publishing one or two books. Jennifer, along with thousands of others with exceptional talents and prestigious doctorates, has been forced to seek new dreams and set new goals. It is a shock, of course, but their successes show the rest of us that these changes are possible and even profitable.

These changes take some serious mental and emotional reorganization. When you are about to enter a new stage in your life, recognize that you will need short-term as well as long-term objectives. Some wise person once stated that goals are considered dreams with deadlines. Because you clearly want to turn your new dreams into reality, you will want to recognize potential timetables.

Your short-term goals are to organize your thoughts and to recognize your skills, talents, interests, values, and objectives. As you reflect on these characteristics, you move to the next stage, which is to contact other people who have an influence on your long-term goal of finding a job. The long-term plan, we assume, is to become enormously successful, hold a progressively responsible job, and win the lottery. Or maybe just have a useful, productive, satisfactory, and successful career. Or even several careers. Why not?

Three Skills Categories

You may have a face with perfect bone structure, a smile that would melt the coldest heart, and a body that belongs in *Vogue* or *Sports Illustrated,* but your skills are what will get you into the workplace. (Yes, we all know stories about gorgeous people who get hired strictly as office decoration, also known as "eye candy," but we're not talking about those folks here. We also have heard the hiring manager's mantra, "Just give me a positive and curious personality, I can teach the skills"—and we're big believers in this philosophy.) We've talked about personality, now let's focus on skills.

We have another list for you, another self-evaluation, if you can handle it, that we have compiled to help people organize the categories of their strengths. It isn't conclusive (what list is?), but it's a start.

The three separate categories—communication, managing others, and data/systems—may be used for identification and to aid your work in finding your new position.

Feel free to add to this list, of course, and the more talents you can demonstrate, the more impressive you will sound on your interview.

Job Market

Now that you have a sharp, clear portrait of your traits and skills, what are you going to do with this knowledge? One of the first caveats we must offer is that many of the positions you will research and be interested in often will not mention a doctoral degree as a prerequisite for employment. Please don't let that stop you from considering these areas. Your advanced education will be a huge advantage, unless you meet up with a hiring manager who is intimidated by your credentials.

But then it's up to you to convince him or her that you're a terrific person and can do the job far better than any other candidate because you do have extraordinary talents. Remember, your degree says a lot about your exceptional skills and your "stick-to-it-iveness" before you even get to the interview, and that degree may well get you in the door. Then you can strut your stuff and show what a great employee (or, better yet, manager, supervisor, even CEO) you will be. You may even discover perks of prestige, additional chances for advancement, and opportunities for continued learning and growth (or a company car; that's been known to happen, also).

We cannot list particular job titles for each personality type, of course, not knowing goals, values, family concerns, or the myriad other issues every individual needs to evaluate. We don't even know what area of concentration your "terminal" degree is in! But let's look at some of the fields you might want to consider and a few of the possible careers that might be found in these eight major sections. Depending on your temperament, you may find several areas worth researching. Also, your university career center will have huge books with tiny print listing thousands of job titles and descriptions, but it helps to have an idea of a particular area you find interesting or appealing before you wallow in those.

1. *Communication:* public relations consultant, writer, journalist, entertainer, recruiter (in any field), television newscaster, marketing guru,

COMMUNICATION

Managing Others

Counseling
Interpreting
Recommending
Coaching
Advising
Giving directions
Making decisions
Resolving conflicts
Problem solving
Setting regulations
Adjusting regulations
Enforcing regulations
Developing procedures
Dealing with change
Motivating
Training
Developing talent
Building teams
Managing details
Organizing
Planning
Supervising
Mentoring
Helping

Written Skills

Sending memos
Preparing talks
Writing letters
Writing evaluations
Writing policy
Writing proposals and grants
Designing

Data/Systems

Analyzing
Synthesizing
Coordinating
Compiling
Computing
Comparing
Researching
Projecting
Reviewing
Designing
Photographing
Drafting
Troubleshooting

Verbal Skills

Consulting
Teaching
Lecturing
Listening
Interviewing
Mediating
Negotiating
Public speaking
Persuading
Presenting ideas
Solving problems
Asking for solutions
Brainstorming
Asking questions
Giving directions
Interpreting ideas

Computer skills, such as Access, Lotus, SDS, UNIVAC, UNISYS, Windows 95/98/2000, Word, WordPerfect, Excel, Power Point, Quicken, or any of the many other programs available, and the creation of Web pages.

project manager, and, of course, teacher, trainer, and consultant in anything you are able to communicate well.

2. *Counseling/Consulting:* career/personal/guidance counselor, psychologist, social worker, hospital administrator/patient advocate, trainer, program designer, change management consultant (popular with the significant downsizing and restructuring of businesses in our current economic climate).

3. *Business*—Entrepreneurial: marketing wizard, organizational developer, sales manager, employment specialist, inventor (as in invent your own position), team builder, diversity trainer, real estate broker.

4. *Business*—Finance: telecommunications administrator, economist, banker, financial planner, planning and development expert (cities, local, and national), stockbroker, estate planner, credit analyst.

5. *Creative Adventures:* photographer, writer, agent, inventor, entertainer, business owner, realtor, travel writer, alligator wrestler, or bricklayer (don't laugh—we heard about one of each of those last two, both with doctorates).

6. *High Tech:* anything to do with computers/technology or telecommunications in which you feel comfortable. The main criteria are curiosity, willingness to learn, a brain with strong left side logic/analytical abilities and incredible right side creativity, unstructured time schedules, and a willingness to let your irreverent side pop out when least expected.

7. *Human Services:* human resources professional, teacher, superintendent, administrator in any level or arena of human services, which includes hospitals and clinics, all sizes and flavors of businesses . . . any place where you run into people. We suppose that leaves out veterinarian offices and maybe mortuaries, but those have a few people, and, anyway, you get the idea.

8. *Marketing:* public relations master, creative director, strategic planner, publicist, superb researcher, sales virtuoso, customer service director/trainer.

Obviously, there are zillions more jobs and job descriptions, but our only goal is to pique your interest. Now we want to tell you about the one area you probably will encounter first and the first folks you will deal with in your job search. They are the heartbeat of most organizations, and you will encounter them many times during employment. You'll also get to know them during termination, which we trust will be voluntary.

Human Resources

Human resource folks are everywhere. They are like the computerized television ads showing 1,001 bouncing babies—only it's the same bouncing baby repeated as many times as the page will hold the image. You simply cannot escape a human resource department, but you probably don't want to—the HR staff may become your best ally, your finest resource, or even your future place of employment. They can be found in big offices near the entrance of any business or tucked away in a quiet corner behind tall, gray partitions. No matter where their office is, they function as the heartbeat of any institution, and you probably are on a first-name basis with many HR people of your own university.

In case you have wondered what exactly these people do beside hand out forms, we found a lighthearted description tacked to the bulletin board of a local human resource department. No one claimed responsibility for it, but we enjoyed assuming it might be one of their training guides.

Maybe it would be a good idea for you to know your areas of expertise so you won't be placed in the wrong office . . . but then, you should be applying to a specific position, which would avoid the "What in the world do we do with this smart person?" dilemma. Of course, you are that smart person, but you absolutely must have a position in mind when you walk in the door.

Some career advisers or well-meaning friends will advise you to avoid the human resources department at all costs and go directly to the decision makers of your potential department. We've been told that works in some industries, but in others you have no choice: You must enter through the human resource door. Many times your résumé will not be considered unless it is sent to HR first, and HR is usually the office that directs résumés to the appropriate decision makers and keeps résumés on file for future reference. So you may wish to go directly to the hiring manager, but this choice may not be yours. Don't argue with the individual system; just know that different offices have different methods.

Now, because a sense of humor is vital to every life, let's add a few more tips for you to tuck under your hat that may be pulled out, magically, when the situation demands some creativity.

HUMAN RESOURCE GUIDE

Place all prospective employees together in a room containing only one table and two chairs. With no instructions, leave them there for two hours. At the end of the two hours, return to the room and see what they have been doing.

If they have taken apart the table and chairs, assign them to Engineering.

If they have counted the scratches in the table, put them in Finance.

If they are screaming and waving their arms, send them to Manufacturing.

If they are talking to the chairs, they belong in Personnel.

If they are sleeping, they are Management material.

If they are writing about the experience, send them to Technical Publications.

If they ignore you when you walk in, they're perfect for Security.

If they try to tell you nothing is as bad as it looks, send them to Marketing.

If they've left early, put them in Sales.

Writing Tips for the Business World

Every academic learns early in graduate school to follow the tenet that pretentious and obscure writing equals good writing. They are joined by the traditional computer manual writers, whose writing styles are as obscure as any we can imagine. But, in general, overblown language is not wanted in the business world. The motto in business often has been stated as "Fuzzy writing reflects fuzzy progress; clear concise writing catapults careers." Why say "A large portion of the interface coordination communication must utilize and be functionally interwoven with the sophisticated hardware" when you could say "The two systems need to talk and respond to each other"?

As you know, each industry seems to have a language all its own. Strong writing, however, bridges all industries, and we encourage you to keep your love of good grammar, a well-turned phrase, and a smooth writing style. You may want to revisit some of the books on your shelf you have used in the

REFERENCES ON WRITING

The Elements of Style (1999, 4th ed.), William Strunk, Jr., & E. B. White (Englewood Cliffs, NJ: Prentice Hall)

The Little English Handbook (1998), Edward P. J. Corbett & Sheryl L. Finlke (Reading, MA: Addison-Wesley/Longman)

Style: Ten Lessons of Clarity and Grace (1999), Joseph M. Williams (Reading, MA: Addison-Wesley/Longman)

On Writing Well (1990), William Zinsser (New York: Harper Perennial)

Woe Is I (1996), Patricia O'Conner (New York: Putnam)

Words Into Type (1974), Marjorie E. Skillin & Robert Malcolm Gray (Englewood Cliffs, NJ: Prentice Hall).

The Well Tempered Sentence, A Punctuation Handbook for the Innocent, the Eager, and the Doomed (1983), Karen Elizabeth Gordon (New York: Ticknor & Fields)

past, but in case you would like a brush-up, a few of the time-honored books on writing skills are listed above.

To give you a jump-start on understanding the world of business, commerce, free-wheeling financial structures, or whatever you wish to call the real world, we are adding what is popularly referred to as a "Short Course on Business Writing." You can find many lists of similar hints in magazines and books, but this will save you some time. These "top ten" tips are valuable for any writing, not just writing for the "business" world.

Now that your big picture writing is on track, we would like to add a word of caution about lingo and slang. As we mentioned, every profession, business, or segment of operations seems to invent its own particular language. Some are so intricate that only the insiders understand the meanings, and even they may have trouble if they change departments.

We realize specialized terminology is necessary to produce whatever work is being done, but we also find a trend toward overblown, puffy language that reminds us of people writing only to make an impression, regardless of the nonsense meanings. Some of the terms make sense; others remind that there are still folks who love to sit around at coffee breaks playing word games to stump fellow workers.

TOP TEN LIST OF WRITING RULES

1. Know your audience—size, gender, culture—as well as how many will be attending: a department, the entire company, or only one or two coworkers. Aim your material to your audience.

2. Good writing reflects good thinking. Because you need to be clear on what you want to say before you can write it, construct an outline. All writing, even a memo, is a story with a beginning, middle, and end. If you know where you want to end up, your message will progress smoothly and make sense. It may be only three sentences, but write them in logical order.

3. Write like you talk—but only if you are a person who can get a point across clearly, quickly, and succinctly. If you are a babbler, write like you would like to talk.

4. Eliminate jargon and buzzwords unless absolutely necessary! We know every industry has its own language, but keep it to a minimum (see the list on page 63 for common business buzzwords to know, but avoid them in writing if possible).

5. Rewrite! No one gets it right the first time. Edit to tighten. Eliminate every unnecessary word. Use a thesaurus and a dictionary for word searches. Short is powerful.

6. Active language. Not "The effort was put out by the marketing department" but "We introduced the product." Passive puts people to sleep.

7. Emphasize key points with bullets, set off with wider margins.

8. Have someone else edit your work. What's clear to you may not be clear to readers.

9. Let it sit for a few hours or overnight, especially if you wrote when angry or in an emotional turmoil. Then take out the emotion and keep the message on an intellectual level.

10. Read it aloud. If it sounds right to your ears, it will read right by others, and you will pick up any little glitches.

The rapid business and technological advances of the 1990s helped inspire some interesting and creative new words, which seem to be finding their way into everyday conversations. Many people think these words are pure slang or perhaps even lazy speech; others love them and toss them around at every opportunity. We doubt if you would find these words in the reference books mentioned previously—but some of them may be appropriate for certain audiences.

Others surely can be used for adding a light touch to your speeches when humor is needed or sprinkled into your conversations to see if others are actually listening. We only put them here to let you know what fun, and to warn you what nonsense, exists in the business world.

We don't want to scare you off from this big world outside the ivory tower; we want to assure you that with a sense of humor and all your terrific language and writing skills, you are bound to have a lot of fun exploring the various languages of business.

Branding—A Hot (Pun Intended) New Concept

As a brief overview of the first four chapters, we would like to share the concept of *branding*, which is simply a way (as said previously) of distinguishing yourself from competitors. The term has a strong visual and mental impact and has become popular among those who offer advice for various areas of work. Whether these advice-givers call themselves career counselors, guidance counselors, trend evaluators, life change consultants, or quick-change artists, they are in the business of helping others learn how to recognize and focus on talents that respond well to a rapidly changing working world.

There is a book by Tom Peters, prolific writer of management issues, called *The Brand You* (1999), which gives extensive descriptions of the rapidly changing workforce and how we need to distinguish ourselves to be successful in our job searches and future work. Peters feels that about 80% of current white-collar jobs will soon be in jeopardy because technology advances are eliminating the need for people. We all have seen that trend increasing in the past few years. Just try to call the phone company or any large organization, and you may wait for hours to talk to a real person. You could even conclude a lengthy transaction without ever hearing a live, lilting, real-person voice.

Branding, according to Peters, is a way of marketing ourselves by making sure we have a portfolio of significant accomplishments that earn us bragging

---

A SHORT LIST OF NEW BUSINESS LINGO

Actualized
Administrivia
Beyond loyalty (huh?)
Brainstorming/blamestorming
Branding (distinguishing self
    from competitors)
Contingent workforce
Core competencies
Customer-focused; customer-
    centric
Declutter, devalue, detweak,
    defocus
Discontinuous change
Downsize, upsize, rightsize
E-commerce, e-trade, e-business
Empowerment
Equivalent
Excel
Excellence
Functional silos (departments)
High-performance
Maximarketing

Multitasking
Outside the box,
    inside the box
Outsourcing
Paradigm
Ratchet up/down
Reengineering
Restructuring
Skill set
Synergy
Team building—forming,
    norming, storming,
    forming (quite common in
    companies that are devel-
    oping and building a
    workforce for team projects)
Uninstall
Value-added
Value analysis
Vision/mission (this is a
    common, and logical,
    concept)

---

rights. The best way to secure a position and grow and develop is to make ourselves indispensable. How? By doing the best work we can, by volunteering for extra projects, by being up-to-date on what the Internet can offer, by being a super researcher and networker both in person and on the Internet. We also need to take initiative and speak up to get noticed and articulate our accomplishments with pride.

Additional changing workforce trends include doing less work in the actual office as more travel and mobility are required (home offices are increasing in popularity and efficiency, thanks to our ever-growing technology); a tendency to work on one project until completion rather than trying to do seven things at once; and fewer endless boring meetings, with more company communication by e-mail along with short, focused interactions. Team efforts are increasingly used for specific projects, which sometimes makes it more difficult for one person to get a "brand."

Peters adds some personality traits to his discussion on branding. He feels that people who have made a significant contribution to their world tend to have quite a few personality traits in common, including being willing to take risks, wanting to make things better, focusing on goals, being creative and even quirky, thriving on chaos but remaining tuned into the needs of others, and, one of our favorites, being irreverent. In other words, successful workers self-branded themselves, looked forward, and simply went out with a distinctive and dedicated personality to commit themselves to whatever captured their interest and energy. What wonderful advice for anyone who wants to make a mark and a difference! And what a wonderful concept for doctoral graduates to remember and practice.

We hope these first few chapters have encouraged you or even forced you to take a good look at your amazing talents and how you can use them in the brave new world you are entering. You probably have used up at least four rolls of film by now, so reload your camera and set your lens to an even wider focus as you investigate more options.

Reference

Peters, Tom. (1999). *The brand you.* New York: Knopf.

CHAPTER 5

Investigating Popular Paths
The Profit and Nonprofit Worlds

You have been looking through a wide-angle lens at a broad landscape picture, with some broad market areas from Chapter 4 standing out to capture your scrutiny. This chapter focuses on popular potential career paths in both the for-profit and nonprofit worlds. We discuss three specific areas—high tech, consulting, and publishing—in which grads have created happy and successful self-portraits. These three professions are available in both profit and nonprofit worlds, but we spare you a duplicate discussion and list them in the profit discussion only.

The first, high tech, is mentioned because it is such a booming, exciting, free-for-all environment using a wide variety of creative skills that we feel you already possess. The second is consulting, a field that has lured many doctoral graduates who enjoy the creative challenges, the potential for independence, and the opportunity to help others in a direct way. Publishing, with its many facets and growing opportunities, is the third area and is well known for attracting grads who love the continued creative, writing, and editing processes. This time they are getting paid for their talents, a novel concept for any new grad.

The final business opportunity is in the nonprofit segment, and because there are particular details you want to think about before applying, we have covered this area in greater detail.

If you think you would like to tighten the lens focus a bit and explore the world of the entrepreneur, that subject earned its own chapter and follows this one.

The Bottom Line

During your student years, you probably heard stories that business cares more about the bottom line than about people. The concept might have been discouraging enough to send you flying back to completing applications for the elusive tenured positions of academia, in which you, with your trusty new doctorate, know you would be much happier. After all, academia is known for having ideas matter, intelligence highly valued, and the bottom line ignored.

But universities cannot ignore bottom lines either—you just were too busy to think about it. Universities, like businesses, have varied and demanding financial obligations, and you could have heard the same business-minded song in many corners of the campus. Whether it is fund-raising meetings, trustees, and administrators trying to contain runaway costs or deans begging for increased budgets to enlarge staff and faculty, the song is the same: Show me the money.

Besides not hearing the money woes, you also may not have been exposed to significant help or suggestions about researching careers in the "real world," in which both money and talent are talked about openly. One source, who understandably prefers to remain anonymous, mentioned that alternative careers are often considered "devil's work" by academics.

Tenured faculty recognize student abilities and expect, even urge, these talented young people to continue with their intellectual work and become gifted professors, in spite of the dearth of openings. Please understand that nonacademic careers do not mean a nonintellectual career, although that idea has been mentioned more times than we care to report.

Some professors simply will not budge from their "academia is the only acceptable career path" stance. One George Washington University doctoral candidate went to her committee chair for some career advice. The response—"What can you do?"—jolted her at the time, but maybe the professor did her a favor. She does have to figure out and be able to articulate clearly what skills she brings to the business world. This young woman and many grads need to load their cameras with faster-speed film and an extended zoom lens as they examine nonacademic careers.

Business—Profit

Let's be realistic. The business world is very different from the world of academia. "The academic culture is myopically focused on itself and does not address the same issues as business," said a successful stockbroker, a Ph.D. graduate. You know this by now. But do you know that businesses often consider doctoral graduates to be dreamers, isolated from market forces and lacking team experience? This can be a hefty drawback for job seekers, trying to convince interviewers that they can follow business expectations by being productive, are able to abide by deadlines, and will help show a profit. Employees are expected to perform on time and within time schedules and to collaborate smoothly and productively with team members—often a challenge to any independent-minded worker, not merely a refugee from academia.

If you have spent adolescence and your early—or extended—adulthood in the ivory tower, you are familiar with occasional professorial patterns of disregarding schedules set (or requested) by their students. Unfortunately, students often have little success in challenging the system. Did you give your adviser chapters of your dissertation that were not returned for weeks or even months after you announced your intended deadline? Do you remember dissertation defense dates shifting around, not because you were not ready, but because the committee had not yet read your work? You are not likely to find such a "Well, whatever, whenever" attitude in business. Deadlines are not easily shifted if that business is to remain viable and profitable. The rumors you heard about business not caring about people have some basis. Businesses are for-profit because otherwise they would sink like a rock in a pond. Why do you think the figures for successful small businesses claim that only 1 out of 10 survive? If a business does not make money, there may be many reasons. A poor business plan, inefficient strategies, not understanding their particular market, tough competition, employees with sticky fingers in the till—whatever the reasons (aka excuses)—they are soon out of business.

High-Tech Industry

The first business environment, and also one of the most exciting and highly visible ones, is the high-tech industry. You might want to do some serious research here. If the potential to make big money is important to you and you think you would thrive in a cutting-edge, fast-paced environment, you might want to look into the exploding technology world. This industry typically pays well, offers interesting work, and has many openings for creative and hard-working people with your talents. This field definitely appreciates your multiple skills as a doctoral graduate.

You need technical skills, but you do not have to be a wizard or *Wunderkind*. We always think of engineers as having highly prized technical skills, but companies are not typically run by engineers; they are run by profit-oriented owners (who also answer to stockholders), creative entrepreneurs, and managers who keep everything running smoothly. Doctoral graduates have the talents to survive beautifully in this commercial world. You have strong communication, writing, presenting, motivating, analyzing, organizing, and other flexible skills needed to help a company continue to build profits. These positions are prized by those who enjoy a fast-paced, creative, and changing world.

We spoke with one woman concerned that her job for a wireless company did not reflect her high level of education. However, the job was her entry into the industry. She was confident that once she was working on the inside, she would have the opportunity to meet others in her company and others in the industry and that her career would advance more easily because of her well-developed skills.

This woman started her job search methodically. She used her extensive networking skills. Her positive attitude and her ability to follow through—with follow-up phone calls and thank-you notes—expressed her interest in finding a job and proved that she would be a valuable worker. She arranged informational interviews even when she had to fly several hundred miles away. She was correct in not limiting herself to job interviews; her informational interviews revealed further knowledge that she could use to impress those hiring. She stated, "One never knows where one interview will lead. Never turn down an opportunity."

Interestingly, this woman felt there was less discrimination toward women than in other areas of work. Perhaps the newness of her specialty and the younger age of people working in this industry make for a more nondiscriminatory workplace. Her present job requires extensive travel in the

United States and South America, and she is confident that her high-tech career will continue to be satisfying.

Consulting Firms

Consulting is a second business area in which many doctoral grads find a lucrative home. You are a good communicator, and the ability to communicate is central to any consulting work. An East Asian languages and civilizations Ph.D. graduate took her degree and went to work for Booz-Allen & Hamilton. Like others, she was no longer interested in academic life after having spent so many years in that environment, and she was eager to move into a world in which she could set her own fees, schedule her own hours, and get rewarded personally and financially for her creative work.

Consulting firms usually offer a team environment or the opportunity eventually to pursue individual accounts. Both areas desperately need people, organization, and creative skills. Whatever your personality—introverted, extroverted, or if you can fire up either talent at will—there is most likely a consulting firm that would benefit from your skills.

You can always go out and start your own consulting organization, as did a leadership doctoral graduate we know. She used her talents and experiences to establish a work environment that is both challenging and productive. We have heard of several individuals who have chosen this entrepreneurial path, and although there are possible pitfalls as with any small business (big businesses, too, for that matter), the benefits in independence and control of time and schedules often outweigh negative aspects. The biggest negative is usually lack of a steady and dependable paycheck, but retainer fees, creative marketing, and determination to build a power base tend to resolve that issue for many entrepreneurs. (The next chapter is stuffed with entrepreneurial ideas.)

Another graduate used his education as a launching pad for becoming an expert witness, and then he established his own consulting firm. He confessed to charging "astonishing" fees for his time, fees that he never would have garnered if he had remained solely in academia. His academics and advanced degrees are enormously respected and remain his ticket to an emotionally and financially satisfying career.

Publishing Companies

The publishing world, with all its broad offerings, is another area worthy of your investigations. Publishing remains a popular career choice for many escapees from academia, and it should be seriously considered by those who feel their talents are best expressed in a research, writing, editing, and/or public relations world. There are many publishing companies, of all sizes and genres, and new ones are sprouting up all the time to respond to growing demands. In addition, the booming world of Internet publishing has inspired many companies to set up new divisions to be a part of this explosion. Opportunities abound.

Business—Nonprofit

The world of nonprofit has many similarities to the profit-based world, and your career search should include both environments. As in our discussion of high tech, consulting, and publishing, most of this information applies to both for-profit and nonprofit worlds. There are a few differences, however, and it's time to touch on those.

Nonprofit organizations can work in almost any community segment and may include foundations focused on health care, education, scholarships, research organizations, and child development—you name it, there's an organization. One of the benefits of nonprofits includes knowing you are working in an important "people" area, an aspect you may find an agreeable and suitable substitute to academia.

Be aware, however, of a couple of significant differences from working in a for-profit career. The first and most obvious challenge is the fund-raising aspect, which can present an almost constant push to find and capture new financial support. If you are gutsy, can ask for money and/or support on a regular basis, or enjoy blending talents with active fund-raisers, you will love this work. You may report to a board instead of a boss, and we all know that the more people in a room making decisions, the more confusing and long-winded the process may be. (This advice comes, with a wink, from a veteran of the nonprofit sector.)

Nonprofit employees are considered to be in two very different groups. The first is management-oriented. This sector typically does not require advanced degrees and includes public relations and fund-raising specialists, competent office workers who keep the rest of us organized and able to do our work, as well as accountants and lawyers. Often, a nonprofit organization trains people to counsel others in need, volunteers to aid disaster victims, teachers to teach literacy to adults, and volunteers to help people attain a GED, among others. The management-oriented group is on the front line and important to any nonprofit organization.

The second group includes people who specialize in specific areas and have spent many years adding to their knowledge in graduate programs and writing dissertations. Child-centered programs, physical and mental abuse problems, health-related programs, senior citizen concerns, and international problems are only a few of the areas covered by nonprofit organizations.

Foundations appreciate and seek out expertise in given areas, but they also recognize and insist that their employees have the ability to write and be competent researchers. People in foundation work also recognize that doctorates are often necessary for upward progression. Therefore, employees working in nonprofits know that if they want to advance their careers, they must return to school for the doctoral degree. You have that degree; you are ahead of this game.

Nonprofit Hiring

Entering the nonprofit world has similarities to the business world, but during the interview process there will be many questions regarding your dedication to the purpose of that particular organization. For example, if you are interviewing for the Ford Foundation, make sure you match your area of expertise with an area of concern that the foundation is known for or hiring for at this time.

A common question that you will be asked concerns your dissertation chair and the work of the particular school you attended. The feeling in foundation work is that your dissertation should not be abstract, but of substance. "Are they doing great things?" is the implied message, and, of course, you will quickly answer, "Yes indeed!" What examples can you give concerning your interest? How does your dissertation tie in with this particular foundation, or how can you stretch it to fit smoothly?

Because research is often a big segment of foundation work, you will be viewed as being given an opportunity to continue your love of research and make a significant contribution. Your dissertation research should be on the cutting edge (too late now to change it, so think fast on this one); be specific and consider various options. There are likely several implications, and you need to know the positive as well as any negative ones. How can these implications be used by the foundation? What are the different applications?

Obviously, your skills and discipline must be linked with the foundation. If you have the same skills and area of expertise as do others in the nonprofit, you may not appear to be as interesting. Set yourself apart. Perhaps you have thought about something they have not considered. Perhaps you were given the opportunity to consider another aspect of a similar problem but came to a different solution. However, you have additional knowledge and that also could be discussed.

Another aspect of the application process is determining how your focus can fit into the large picture. Often, students choose a very narrowly defined problem and concentrate on the immediate concern. When working in academia, you have been forced to consider some fairly small issues. But how does that issue apply to the world? Your last dissertation chapter likely gave you the opportunity to discuss the implications and recommendations of your dissertation. If you discussed a large picture, you will find this step easier now.

As the saying goes, be prepared to "think outside the box." This is clearly the time to speak up about the large issues involved with your work. What makes your work unique and useful to the foundation? How can your information be used in additional ways?

Research the Organizations

Remember our suggestion to do thorough Internet research on many different companies? This includes nonprofits. In particular, what does the mission statement say about the organization, and how does it relate to the way you feel about yourself and your abilities? You need to be able to speak articulately on why you feel working for any organization, profit or nonprofit, will be of immense benefit to them. (Yes, yes, it will benefit you also, of course. But any organization wants to know first what you can do for them.)

You can never know too much about an organization before an interview. For the nonprofits, you will want to know the history and how long they have been around. A new nonprofit has advantages for you starting on the ground floor and hopefully advancing as the organization grows. An older foundation is likely to be well established and well known, but it is probably also well staffed with few or no openings. Funding for the established foundations tends to be attractive, however, as the historical perspective often impresses old as well as new donors.

Funding is essential for the nonprofit world. Because nonprofits do not make something for a profit, there have to be other avenues of paying the bills. Find out: Are there repeat donors? Are there large fund-raisers? Is the government funding the organization? Does the nonprofit rely on many small donations that can change with the economic times? Will any of this affect your future job? How secure is the nonprofit? Do you care? What is the culture like? Is it open, friendly, supportive, communicative at all levels, and open to new ideas, or do they tend to operate behind big oak doors with closed mouths and minds?

What is the size of the organization? Just as with any business, organization size affects your status in the overall work picture. Do you like to work in large organizations in which you can blend in, or do you want to stand out immediately and make a real difference?

When considering work with a nonprofit, know yourself and make some decisions. What is the purpose of the nonprofit? What is the culture of the organization? What does the nonprofit offer the world and you? What do you want? Is there common ground? Is this a good match?

Some Reminders for Both Profit and Nonprofit Positions

When you complete an interview and decide that you are not interested in any job at that particular organization, there is no reason to burn bridges. Remember the possibility of networking. Both business environments may have suggestions that will steer you to the perfect job somewhere else. "I was stunned when I was not immediately hired," stated one recent and happily employed graduate. "I was a perfect fit. Little did I know that the president of the foundation was having dinner that night with the head of human resources at another foundation and would recommend me for another position."

One last reminder: The old rules about thank-you notes are still golden. Always write thank-you notes. The organization spent time reviewing your résumé and interviewing you; let them know you appreciate their consideration. Mention your continuing interest in the organization, your pleasure in meeting others during your interview (sure hope you remembered to write down their names), the culture of the organization that you particularly enjoy, and the ease with which you could move to the new location, if that is true.

Perhaps you did not answer a question well, and you have stewed about it ever since walking out the door. In a letter, clarify your thoughts so that people at the organization know that you have a better response and are still interested. Follow-up calls can be made but, because you do not want to be known as a pest, space them out to weekly or every 10 days or so. If you receive a rejection, you still want to acknowledge receiving the letter and that you hope the organization finds someone to satisfy their expectations. You do not know if you are second in line and the first person may not take the position.

Salary

You know that business is oriented to the bottom line; you may not be aware that the nonprofit organizations are more sensitive when it comes to salary. When money is raised from outside sources, nonprofits cannot allow themselves to be perceived as squandering money on salaries instead of using their money for their stated purpose.

On the other hand, you need to eat too, and strong negotiation skills will help you achieve a satisfying balance between the work of the organization and their ability to pay you. Also important are the fringe benefits. Perhaps the benefits are superior to another job opening. Carefully check all the details of an offer, because the actual salary is only one part of the total package. Then review: Is there a commitment that brings you together? Are your values and interests the same?

If you decide the nonprofit route is the one you wish to take, you will find plenty of material, such as lists of foundations and organizations, on the Internet, in business magazines, and even in your phone book. It is an area worthy of your exploration, for these organizations offer valuable and interesting choices, and you will often discover other former academics who share similar yearnings for reaching out to help others.

Changing Perceptions

Even though there is a perception inside academia that business communities are not interested in scholarly concerns, there is a growing trend among tenured faculty to rethink that stand. Foundation work is probably more easily accepted among faculty because of the good deeds, the continued research necessary to foundation work, and the reluctance of foundations to pay huge salaries. Business may be oriented to the bottom line, but there are many that are also community-minded, that are considerate of ecological systems, and that treat their workers fairly. We also need the world that business provides. As one graduate said, "It's refreshing to be in a [business] world that has market forces, because no one is kidding you that there are audiences that you have to sell to and dirty politics." Business tends to be more blunt about realities, and will easily "tell it like it is."

We encourage everyone to make a choice that is right for him or her. If your choice is academia, fine, this is a vital and desperately needed resource for us all. If you want to go into the business sector, either profit or nonprofit, that's great too. But please do not let anyone in academia try to hold you back or discourage you from your desires to move on, just as no one in business has a right to discourage you from changing companies or even returning to academia. In most communities, the academic, business, and nonprofit foundations cooperate enthusiastically and increasingly efficiently for the benefit of all concerned. That's the best of all worlds.

The point is that your academic skills can be used in multiple situations. The abilities to analyze, write, and communicate are never unappreciated endeavors. Your skills were developed over many years. Now is the time for you to decide how they can be used best and to find the greatest way for you to live your life.

CHAPTER 6

Exploring Entrepreneurial Options

This May Be Your Golden Opportunity

There's another career option in our multi-optioned world that may be attractive to you if you have a creative, independent-minded, open-to-risk streak that begs to be satisfied—the growing world of entrepreneurship. Call it what you will, "doing it myself," "going my own way," or simply "my turn," it's all the same. As one entrepreneur of an auto agency stated in a typical automotive metaphor, "I love being the creator, the motor, the fuel, and the driver. I'm in charge." If this personality fits you, read on.

First, we'd like to share what is known as the "Entrepreneur Mind Set." There seems to be a particular personality drawn to this challenging career path, with primary attributes of being undaunted by risk, obsessed with opportunity, fueled by creativity, and willing to put in long hours. Entrepreneurs also seem to need high energy and to have a dedication to a dream, a plan to take to a bank if a small (or any size) business loan is needed for start-up funding, or even a solid understanding of how "VC"—venture capital—works if you have a grand idea worthy of grand funding. If you fit any of these descriptions and are still interested, stick around. We have learned a few pearls that may help you get started, but if you wish to know more, take some business classes or start serious reading about the business world.

New doctoral graduates tend to voice two main concerns: "What would I do?" and "How will I be able to start it up?"

Many business advice books break down an entrepreneur path into about six categories to give you something to think about before flinging yourself blindly into the market. We have included most of the main topics here, mostly as an introduction to ideas for you to ponder.

Exploring Your Interests

Gathering Research/Information

Writing a Business and Marketing Plan

Analyzing Potential Risk

Putting the Pieces Together

Hiring Helpers and Advisers

Exploring Your Interests

"What can I do if I don't teach?" is the common wail springing from the academically saturated brains of postdocs. By now, if you've read the previous chapters, you know you have strong market value. We know (and eagerly credit you for) your exceptional organizational, research, and written skills. The only obstacle (besides an ever-blooming money tree) may well be a lack of confidence in the business realm, probably due mostly to lack of exposure. Perhaps you have had no time to consider these free-ranging options, but here we try to give you a general idea.

The following short list offers quick snapshots of areas that may remind you of an earlier, or a newly developed, passion or interest. We have grouped four general categories to consider: Retail, Service, Consulting, and Marketing/Advertising. (There are others, of course, but this is a chapter, not a book, so we are only hitting the highlights that might appeal to you and get you thinking outside the academic box. If you are interested in this path, you will find many detailed, opinionated, and/or mind-boggling books in the business section of your local library, bookseller, or university bookstore.)

Gathering Research/Information

Create a list of industries that spark your interest, and then go over it carefully, collecting and culling ideas, to see what makes your intellectual fires burn. When you narrow the list to a few favorite areas, start gathering all the information you can, because you will be pouring enormous time, energy,

---

Retail: Concepts to Consider

Anything from appliances to zoo food is a potential business.

Any product that offers something people need, want, and are willing to pay for is potentially viable.

The first crucial step is to analyze the market and range of competitors.

Retail details are extensive, so do your homework! Location, expenses, product shipping, staffing, advertising, and growth potential all must be considered.

The best plan is to begin by interviewing others who have started businesses, and then listen to all the positive and negative feedback.

Service: Points to Ponder

The world economy is becoming more service-oriented; would the following aspects appeal to me?

There is less capital expenditure—usually far less.
I can start locally, gradually build to national, even international.
The only inventory to maintain will be my own materials.
My brains, skills, and communication talents are worth compensation.
Payment is usually prompt, and can be requested prior to service.

There are many varied arenas available, including (but certainly not limited to) customer service, consulting, tutoring, time management, organizational techniques, train-the-trainers, public speaking, computers, and management.

Consulting: Areas to Explore

There are many potential areas for consultants; you will want a primary area of focus, but you can easily expand into new areas with minimum research.

Think big picture: what do you know best? Do you want to stay in the academic realm? If so, anything from grade school to grad school is open to you.

Are you a whiz on computers? This field is desperate for trainers at all levels.

Can you coach, mentor, train, teach, encourage? The world is busily creating different terms, but they are strikingly similar concepts. Pick one you like best.

Explore mental health, management techniques, leadership training, and sports psychology. Let your imagination run wild here.

The advantages are many: no inventory, no required office rental (home offices are booming), and no one to depend on but yourself. If you grow, you are still in charge. What a nice feeling that is!

Successful consultants are those who have spent time in the marketplace, like to be in charge (a "director" we know laughingly refers to herself as "dictator", because "I love being in charge—finally—of my own life and future!"), enjoy working alone or in small groups, have written books or manuals on their subject, give talks and speeches at every opportunity, and have a large network of professional contacts.

Marketing/Advertising: Where Ideas Go to Get Paid

This is a booming area for the extroverted and energetic folks who love being around people and who can sell ice cubes to Alaskans or boogie boards to Nebraskans.

Powerful marketing can make almost any product or idea sound like the hottest bargain in town. For example, can you imagine why anyone would buy a "pet rock," or land under a Florida swamp?

Those of you with creative writing skills may find a rich vein of writing opportunities in almost any industry, including publishing, public relations, ghostwriting, political speech writing, and freelance venues such as magazine writing and editing.

Think big—but get a day job until you land on your financial feet.

heart, and money (yours or someone else's) into your new adventure. You will live, breathe, eat, dream about, and sweat over this new entity. Talk to owners of big and small businesses, asking as many questions as you can dream up. Ask about everything from time to money to heartache to thrills to organizational needs to advertising to how in the world did they even think up the business in the first place.

One woman we spoke with began her career as a freeway flyer, dashing from one university to another, teaching part-time but never knowing if she would have a class the next semester. She was always interested in business. Her father owned a stationery store, and she often had helped out during busy times, but she was never even asked if she was interested in becoming part or full owner.

When a health problem jolted her dad's complacency, he decided to sell the store, but not, of course, to his daughter. After all, he reasoned stubbornly, she was an academic—a frustrated academic, but nonetheless hardly a businesswoman. You can guess the ending of this story. . . . She is now the owner and manager of a very successful and growing stationery and office supply store, with expansion goals on the drawing board. She says her organization (keeping the books), writing (store advertising), and people skills (joining women's and small business networks) are building her business. It doesn't hurt that the nearby community college deals almost exclusively with her organization. Similar backgrounds, you know.

Did she need a doctorate to do this? Of course not. But it doesn't hurt, and it gives her prestige and credibility. "People are impressed by the initials," she says with a smile, "and no one ever asks about my major."

Not many of us have built-in business opportunities to fall into, and some of us who do choose not to go that direction. Two friends of ours turned thumbs down to family-owned businesses, saying they preferred the tranquil "life of the mind" in ivory halls to the rough-and-tumble world of commerce. To fill in time while searching academia, they worked in family businesses. When the first solid paychecks came in, neither ever looked back. Because they loved the academic realm, however, their businesses have formed partnerships with local colleges to offer internships and student support. They also enjoy giving an occasional guest lecture to entrepreneurial classes. This is a trend happening with many universities and local communities, and it is beneficial for both.

Another terrific source for research is an organization called SCORE—the Service Corps of Retired Executives. This organization has been operating and expanding since 1964 and has offered ideas, suggestions, workshops, and moral support to more than 3 million business owners and to more entrepreneurs than we can begin to count. Here is the best news: It's free. Other best news: There are almost 400 chapters across the United States. You can find a chapter close to you by calling your local Small Business Administration office or hopping on the Internet (www.score.org).

Writing a Business and Marketing Plan

Why do you need a business plan? Mainly to get money, if you need financing, and who doesn't? Copies may go to your banker, your attorney, and even to friends who may be able to help you (but not to competitors), and main ideas certainly will be discussed among potential employees. You must write it, so start planning.

"A business plan is like an interview," insisted a venture capitalist, "you have one to two minutes to get my attention. I like them short, but complete. Well written, not wordy. Well organized, not sloppy. And you better be pitching a good idea or I'm not interested, now or ever."

Hello? Doesn't this sound a bit familiar? Well written, well organized, creative? Sell your ideas to a room full of strangers? Of course you can do this, these are your strengths! To make sure, however, do your homework: Get several books on how to write business and marketing plans from your local library, business school, bookstore, or off the Internet, because academia certainly did not prepare you for the homework you will need to do for this critical component. As you continue reading general ideas here, however, you will note many similarities to dissertation preparation, which may offer a smidgen of comfort.

We read that in 1997 (the most recent figures available), more than $10 billion was invested by venture capitalists into businesses they felt had strong potential. All you have to do is scan the newspaper or watch business reports on television to know that this figure has grown significantly and will continue to do so, particularly in a strong economy. And yes, tech businesses are all the rage now, but every other area is worthy of your consideration as well.

Our research indicates a basic business plan has at least four main sections: summary, background, current status of your business, and a customer analysis, including your current and potential competition. We are not going to give you a blow-by-blow here, but, like you, we can read and interview.

And we have one industrious friend who helps people write business plans for fun (and big bucks), can you imagine? Maybe this is a new career for you, as well.

Here is what we found about the four sections:

Summary

Aim for one page, five paragraphs. The first paragraph is an overview, the second reports what makes you different from your competition, the third offers the results of your market testing and research to date, and the fourth contains your qualifications and the expertise of any others on board. The final paragraph reveals your current financial status, investors, and loans, and you may even have to admit to buying lottery tickets, although we personally don't think that would be a wise topic to discuss.

Background

Describe your business and what sets it apart from other businesses that are similar in concept and size. You will need to include a bunch of marketing research for this one, which means more than running your fingers through the yellow pages.

Current Status of Your Business

This indicates where you are right now—on the drawing board, starting, have been up and running for awhile, and so on. Do you have a name, logo, and product, and if so, are they available? For example, how do you plan to make it available? Who manufactures?

Customer Analysis and Competition

You can do your market research here by reporting who your potential customers will be by age, gender, and general interests; then, you discuss your sales strategies of how to reach that market. Analyze your competition and the market share they currently have and why your business would be different or better or more profitable than others.

Does all this information make you want to be a consultant instead, using your brains as the product and your home as an office?

No? Still interested? Okay, let's talk about the other half of this epistle, a marketing plan that tells the world how you plan to produce, sell, and service your future business. Most of the marketing plans we researched had seven sections, at least. Some had more, but this seems to be enough to give you the idea. And plans do not follow this list in the same order, of course. We only hit the high spots.

Section 1:   Evaluate the entire potential market.

Section 2:   Analyze your potential customer base, including your competition and the typical buying patterns of your customers and address why your company would be better than the competition.

Section 3:   Why would your business be better? What do you offer that is different, unique, creative, or salable?

Section 4:   Discuss your position on sales, goals, marketing product, and, as usual, how you are going to pay for all the pieces.

Section 5:   This is your press release: advertising, logo, slogan, message, and your plan for spreading the news about what makes your business more wonderful than others. Go to any trade show; you will see how many gimmicks and promises one company can produce and will learn why the PR business slogan is "we can make a silk purse out of a sow's ear." Also, how will you get your message out? Print media, TV, radio, standing on a street corner waving signs and arrows?

Section 6:   Future projections, plans, and goals. Think big, we're told, not many people will invest in the tiny start-ups unless they are something Internet-based and/or technology-oriented, and although those may not have quite the typically high (80%) failure rate for small businesses, many roadsides are littered with broken start-ups.

Section 7: This is the pro forma, the real basic information. You will
need to research and list all expenses, and they do mean all, as
well as projected expenses. Your accountant will be a big help
here.

Analyzing Potential Risk

Part of your research is to conduct a risk analysis, which you need to be aware
of before you settle on an idea and certainly before you sit down to write a
business and marketing plan. Take a walk on the dark side for a few days as
you gather the numbers. Remember the facts you heard in school that 50%
of doctoral students end up ABD—all but dissertation—and never change
that half-completed status? Small business statistics are even darker: About
80% of small businesses fail within the first 5 years, usually because they have
not planned well or assessed potential risks. Most the time the risks are associated with money—you know, that green stuff, the stuff that makes the
world go around and even has been known to pay off college loans.

Some business advisers sum up the world of risks with the acronym
TIME: You will need Time, Ideas (new), Money, and Energy. It will take
bundles of all four to create a successful business. If you compare starting a
business to building a home, many facets are identical: Start with researching
design and goals, plan for a solid foundation, study and analyze each growth
step. "Then expect the project to cost twice as much as budgeted, and take
three times as long as you planned, before it can even come close to being
declared a success," complained one frustrated entrepreneur whose survival
still depended on his wife's income. There are entire books dealing with risk
analysis and avoidance; he suggested any beginner would be wise to add
"research risk potential" on a to-do list.

Other risks to be expected and taken in stride are insufficient resources,
unknown competitors, changes in technology, changing demand for your
product, and, of course, the inevitable delays, detours, setbacks, and heavy
discussions with advisers. There will be some hair pulling and frustrated cuss-
ing along the way. But there will also be plenty of excitement, creative energy,
hope, and satisfaction. And, with skill and luck, financial success will be your
reward. (If that is your goal.)

Knowing your risks and being able to discuss them, face them, and deal
with them appropriately eventually will earn you another degree, as one
young man said. "A second doctorate," he proclaimed proudly from his real

estate office, "Ea.D., Doctor of Entrepreneurial Adventures." This fellow had one suggestion, aimed particularly for the men out there: "Don't be afraid to ask questions, advice, help, directions!" You may be brilliant, dedicated, energetic, and even drop-dead gorgeous, but if you're from the world of academia, unless you spent a lot of time in business school, you are probably a naive novice in the business world. You often had to "go it alone" in the doctoral program, but now you have a lot of help available. Ask for it.

Putting the Pieces Together

What are the pieces? The details! The little, grubby, sometimes annoying but always critical pieces that help get a business off the ground.

First, where should you have your office? At home? In a rented space? What size should it be? Cost? Location? The trend is toward home offices (the most recent government count claims 33 million employees are working at home as "telecommuters," and they range from bosses to beekeepers). Home offices are perfect for start-ups and certainly cut down on your commute. They are particularly popular with consultants, advisers, associates, mentors, and trainers—those on the service side of business.

Electronics cannot be ignored, of course. No business can run without our ever-growing technology. Plan to close your eyes and breathe deeply when you get the bill for setting up a home office, if that's where you decide to begin operations. You will need a big chunk of finances, as any burgeoning business will require computers, printers, fax machines, phones, cell phones, pagers, a few more things that have not been invented yet, and at least seven miles of connecting cords and quadruple the number of current (sorry, couldn't resist) electrical outlets. Your first employee may well be the neighborhood 12-year-old who can set it all up, trouble-shoot the equipment, and quickly update software when necessary. (She may not know how to spell "retirement benefits," so you're safe for now.)

Second detail: money. Where do you find it, how do you get it, how much do you need, and how do you pay it back? We discuss a little more in the business and marketing plans, but know for now that it is a major topic that will take all your organizational and creative skills.

Third: Do you need office furniture and office supplies? Whether you rent or set up at home, this is another expense to plan for, but it is probably one of your smaller headaches.

Fourth: How do you announce to the world that you are now available? In the academic world you use a curriculum vitae or a résumé; in the business world, you don't have to reveal personal details. There are three primary methods of contacting the world: advertising, marketing, and public relations. You surely know the difference, but here's a hint.

Advertising you pay for. Usually, you write your own copy and pick the date or dates the material will be published. The usual format is to place newspaper and magazine ads, but sometimes brochures are included here. You also may consider pasting your ads on billboards, buses, subways, traveling trucks. . . . You get the point, the possibilities are endless. You pay, they print for the specified length of time in the contract. If you are in the service business, you simply need to get your name out. Write articles, see if you can get interviewed, have a clever business card and post it in appropriate and easily seen sites, and be a guest speaker in community organizations.

Some businesses have networking bulletin boards bursting with individual business cards—have yours be colorful and catchy so it will stand out. We once saw a card in a see-through stiff blue cover that resembled a photo negative, with the drawing of a roll of film where the name and phone number was printed. You knew immediately this was a photographer, who reported a huge increase in business after posting his cards around several communities. A neighboring financial planner has green—the color of money—business cards and receives many inquiries. Aim for what captures the eye and interest of a potential customer.

Marketing is the free-wheeling, fun part of being an entrepreneur, and your imagination can run wild here. Marketing is putting your name or logo on an item that is given away for promotion. Because people seem to love any trinkets they can snag for free, this is a booming concept. The items can be anything, from baseball caps to key chains, from pens to pads of paper, from card decks to candles, from golf balls to postcards to shirts to chocolates to any other item you can dream up within financial reason. T-shirts remain one of the most creative forms, used both as advertising and as marketing gimmicks. If you immediately think up about 30 other potential give-away goodies, maybe you ought to consider a new career as a marketing consultant.

The key to marketing, we're told, is to track the results the best you can. It's like Web sites on the Internet, bragging about the number of "hits" each site receives. Tracking is not easy in giveaways, but it is worth a try.

Public Relations usually involves hiring a professional (be aware that they have significant billing rates and offer no guarantees) to get your name, logo, and product or service out into the world by any means possible. It may appear in the print media, on the radio or television, in trade magazines or anywhere else they can dream up. Remember the words "no guarantees"? That's true—but PR folks are usually energetic, positive professionals and will cheerfully approach anyone who is breathing. Just know that this is probably your most expensive route, but, depending on your business, it also may be your most successful. PR expenses tend to grow in proportion to company size and exposure needs.

There are additional pieces and details that will jump out at you as you travel the entrepreneurial path, but this covers the main points, at least for beginners. "Don't give out all the challenges, we don't want to scare anyone away!" laughed a popular former professor who is currently running a successful private tutoring business out of her home.

Hiring Helpers and Advisers

After hiring your first 12-year-old employee as your computer set-up wizard, you will want to have names of some adult professionals to interview. Most books say your primary advisers will be a banker, an accountant, and an attorney. You'll need a banker for a business account, notary service, Small Business Association loans, direct deposits for employees, and advice. Some banks love to work with entrepreneurs; others won't touch them. Some bankers encourage women entrepreneur accounts; others will sweetly (or not) send you somewhere else. There are about 8 million women business owners, employing more than 18 million people, but many women still have trouble getting business loans. Find a bank that is supportive of you and your venture without concern about your gender. Ask friends and business folks for referrals, and then interview for yourself.

The accountant will figure your taxes and help with long-range planning. He or she may be comfortable with contracts and know more than you ever want to hear about appreciation, depreciation, and even desperation. Interview several. And if you are a woman, make sure you don't hook up with a male accountant who turns out to be a misogynist in disguise. He may give professional advice, but it is not worth the sneers and putdowns. (We've heard this story too many times to discount it, and we have dealt with several ourselves.) Whether you are male or female, simply make sure you and the accountant (and all your advisers) are on the same wavelength and can communicate comfortably and honestly.

The third person in your entrepreneurial arsenal is an attorney, and again we suggest you interview and choose wisely. You may be able to fill out the DBA (Doing Business As . . .) form for a fictional name by yourself, if you go that route, but the rest of your setting up may be mumbo jumbo, as it is to most of us who spent our formative years in academia. Almost all future activities—buying property, leasing space or equipment, hiring employees, considering partnerships, and doing serious financial planning—will depend on competent legal advice from someone you can trust and afford.

As for hiring future employees, you will want to hire people to fit the positions. Look to answer the same questions you would be asked in your own job search: Can this person do the job? Will he or she fit in? and How much will you have to pay for their talents? You'll get more of this information in Chapter 10, but it's something to keep in mind.

One caveat: When considering hiring future employees, please remember that federal laws insist we cannot discriminate on race, ethnicity, religion, gender, disability, or age. When conducting interviews, you cannot even ask questions about these areas. But we must add a synthesis of comments recently heard regarding stereotypes about ages of workers. "My best workers are considered 'older,'" reported one business woman. "They bring valuable experience, are steady workers, and they don't party hearty on work nights." Other business owners have told us they offer internships and starting part-time positions to teenagers, who bring energy, a "can-do" attitude, and a fresh curiosity (as well as some creative costuming) to the workplace, which benefits all parties. These strategies may easily work for you as well.

You now may have thrown up your hands and decided to work for someone else or be a consultant or trainer or expert witness using your exceptional thinking and presenting skills—anything but be an entrepreneur. Therefore, let's move to the next chapter and refocus the camera to examine other critical components in the workforce—gender and culture.

PART III

CHAPTER 7

Recognizing Gender and Cultural Issues

The More Things Change, The More They Stay the Same

The past two decades have produced a mother lode of information about the differences, both genetic and cultural, between the two genders and the many different cultures. Although some researchers cry "Foul!" and refuse to engage in these ongoing discussions for fear of encouraging the "different is deficient" philosophy, the facts remain that there are indeed many differences between the genders, within cultures, and, even more so, among individuals. We'd like to share some basic issues that you may not have encountered before, so this chapter tries to fill in what may be some gaps in your education. It never hurts to be prepared.

For those who continue to insist that we live in a melting pot and should all cheerfully blend into a smooth, tasty concoction of living and working together, we beg to differ. We feel that tossing us all into the same stew and encouraging everyone to lose his or her identity, cultural background, and inherent talents is a recipe for frustration and pain. We prefer to focus on unique talents, inherited/acquired skills, and individual personalities and to search for ways to encourage individual and group productivity.

Now that we have clearly stated our preferences—which are probably glaringly obvious throughout this book—let's put a wide-angle lens on our job-hunting camera—no fuzzy filters or color-enhancing tricks here—and examine some current arguments about gender and culture. We would like all newly minted doctors (of both genders and all cultures, of course) to have a clear picture of the free-for-all real world.

First, the Positive Changes

Being naturally upbeat and cheerful, we're going to start with good news about the world of commerce. And your first consideration remains: How are you going to apply your skills to seeking a position in business? There are five areas we discuss here; surely, you will think of others as your search continues.

First, know that communication will be different, and not necessarily easier. In school, you were handed a syllabus with all expectations precisely spelled out, complete with required texts and readings; you will seldom get such detailed structure in a future position. More likely, you will hear, "We need to figure out some way to resolve this problem. Work on it and get back to me tomorrow." Now is the time to let those creative juices run rampant.

Second, you most likely cannot allow a single deadline to slide. You may have been able to take an "incomplete" in a class and worry about it next semester, or next year, or even 2 years later, but that cavalier attitude will not fly in business. Too many others are depending on your input and on you to carry your share of the load, and serious money may be resting on your production. Your slippin' and slidin' days are over.

Third, you'll find differences in the financial structure outside academia. In researching your financial aspects, you can easily find out what teaching jobs pay at each level and the availability of research funds—which often dry up at the most critical time. You will find similarities with the business world here in that starting salaries may be standard information, but raises, promotions, and bonuses are tied to the bottom line, and those resources can disappear into the night mists as quickly as research money. In fact, your entire department can disappear with the flick of a pen: *Oops,* downsized. *Oh-oh,* merger coming through. *Oh my,* lost a big contract. *Doggone it,* lost that big deal to our competitor. *Help,* bought out and about to be replaced by their people. This happens all the time in business; have you ever heard that kind of talk in university settings?

The fourth consideration is teamwork. You may or may not be comfortable working in teams, as we all recall the focus on individual academic competition for the best grades, professors, schedules, and striving to become valedictorian. We also remember the stories of a few students who would quickly check out of the library the books needed for a certain course, leaving their fellow students high and dry. That selfishness probably won't be tolerated in business. Business trends are moving quickly toward working in teams, having to function well together for a common goal. If your competitive streaks shine brightly from academic strivings, we suggest you focus those spotlights on team members and group endeavors, because what is important is—always—the bottom line. Group efforts produce black, not red, lines.

Fifth, make an effort to learn the corporate language. It is never as precise or critically examined as it was in academia, and each industry and business has a language of its own (see Chapter 4). Some words make no sense whatsoever, and that's half the fun. You must love a challenge if you have a doctorate. Here's a fun one. Listen and learn the foreign words and what they mean (that's usually the hard part, figuring out what they mean) and you'll be trilingual before you know what hit you.

Now, for Some Things That Stay the Same: Is Biology Destiny?

The argument continues and is reflected in all areas of our lives. Some cultures preach the doctrine that men are superior to women simply because of their biology, thus they "deserve more" in the way of career advances and better wages. It certainly is easy to spot the many folks who insist their own culture is superior to all others, no matter what the obtuse or unexplainable rules that govern its people (if you doubt this, you don't read newspapers or watch television news). The "My Way Is Better Than Your Way" mentality seems to be a universal human trait.

The 1990s brought about many changes, both in the workplace and within home and family structures. Most workplaces are now far more open to both genders and all cultures, with environments in companies of all sizes striving toward a more worker- and family-friendly attitude. One problem persists, however, and that is the unequal pay structure. The pay scale remains, in general, about 76 cents to the dollar on female/male wage com-

parisons. The Equal Pay Act was signed in 1963 (see dol.gov/dol.wb/
epcheck.htm), but equal pay remains an elusive goal for women in many
companies and industries (see Appendix B for the most recent comparative
list of pay discrepancies).

An interesting new theory is coming out in books and business magazines and was on the *Nightly News* with Tom Brokaw (on July 8, 1999): Perhaps one of the reasons women are paid less is because they don't ask for more
salary when they are hired. Many women are often reluctant to negotiate in
the hiring discussions, haven't completed their homework on appropriate salary ranges for that position, and simply jump on the first offer. "I don't feel
right about haggling over salary," one woman said. "It's not appropriate." Ah,
but it is appropriate and absolutely necessary! It's also expected to be part of a
salary negotiation, but many women apparently are uncomfortable challenging the numbers. Both men and women have told us they assume they are
making comparable pay to their coworkers with the same job title and experience, but do not do the research to establish what the pay range is for that
position. Even if they discover discrepancies, apparently many women are
not willing to enter a tough negotiation to fight for what their research shows
is a fair salary.

We were initially uncomfortable with this new "blame the women"
trend, but on closer look we felt the argument has merit. Women are well
known in the lower echelons of the business world to take the first position
open to them, and, depending on their personal/family needs and hunger
level, this is understood. Many of these women will accept a position hoping
to be treated fairly during their employment, and often they are. But if they
are not treated equally, how many of them will do the homework to present
their case to human resources or their bosses? Apparently not many. And
we've heard that many midlife women were told, when hired, that they
would receive less pay than the men because the men had children to support
and they needed the money more than the women did! It's sad to hear that
such Neanderthal thinking still exists, but the stories keep popping out of
our research and from others. Sadly, genderism is alive and well.

Depending on your cultural and environmental background, as well as
your personality, you may be the type to grab the first offer and hope for the
best. But we encourage all of you, men and women of all cultures, to understand that, for many positions, negotiation is expected, or certainly an
inquiry about it is expected, and if we are willing to sell ourselves and our talents short, of course someone will take advantage of our naïveté! (For more
information on negotiations, read Chapter 11.)

There are several other issues pertaining to women in the workforce that we might as well discuss here. The first is promotions, and again we're talking about inequities. Many women sit back and wait for them to happen, as did the woman who reported, "I watched male coworkers get promotions, but didn't realize they were asking for more responsibility, making themselves more visible, just making more noise. I had to learn to do those things to get noticed." Another recommendation is to document your accomplishments and be prepared to present them on a yearly basis. Or once a week if you are good at tooting your own horn. Why not? Who else will do it if you don't?

A second issue concerning women is the infamous glass ceiling, which is shattering occasionally but has been reported to turn to cement in some businesses. "Concrete ceilings and sticky floors," reported one woman in upper management in a large manufacturing firm. As she advised, if you are headed for upper management or top corporate spots, take a look at your company track record of promotions, how many women are in near-the-top positions, and assess your own chances. It's no secret that many women are choosing to start their own businesses or initially affiliate with smaller companies that offer significant room for learning, growing, and advancement. You don't need a doctorate to figure out these strategies, but your research talents will be helpful.

Third, fourth, and fifth issues, if you have a family, are the possibilities of relocation, travel, and child care. If one of your highest values is family time, you certainly don't want to be dashing through airports any more than is absolutely necessary, and you will need the best child care you can find. Some companies value their employees, both men and women, enough to provide in-house child care, thus keeping workers in the offices and productive. We recently heard of a large national company that has begun a charter school on company grounds. First reports are that it is enormously successful, and no wonder. Maybe the corporate world will become more family-friendly?

Bottom line: We happen to feel biology is not destiny, although we are surrounded by evidence that biology inspires some frustrating trends in all facets of our world, including business. But biology also creates many interesting and diverse talents that should be recognized and enjoyed. Many gender differences are now understood and accepted, and if you have a sense of humor and are willing to honor your own skills and ambitions, forget about gender—concentrate on talents. And stand up for yourself!

Yes, Virginia, There Is a Difference

Are businesses facing up to this fact? For the most part, yes. Published reports and financial statements of large companies reveal a more evenly distributed balance sheet for men and women, but there are still far more male CEOs than female, and that ratio is changing at a snail's pace. Mattel Toys had a woman leader for several years; Hewlett-Packard just announced a new female CEO, and women are finally being talked about as making a run for becoming president of the United States. Great, huh? Yes—but we can still list them without using too many fingers.

One tool for redistribution of the coin has become popular, and that is the infamous lawsuit. Pick up almost any large newspaper and you will find a report of a gender bias lawsuit being initiated. More than 900 women, current and former employees, are suing Merrill Lynch for economic discrimination. Laurel Bellows, former head of the American Bar Association's Commission on Women, was quoted in the *San Diego Union-Tribune* on March 2, 1999: "[Wall Street] is one of the last bastions of discriminatory treatment and unequal standards in the country. . . . The rest of corporate America seems to have figured out that they benefit from qualified, intelligent women" (p. C2).

A heartening story came out of MIT recently, and although this book is aimed at graduates leaving academia, the same principle for challenging inequities can apply. After realizing the huge ratio of 157 men to 15 women professors, and after discussing other issues such as women being assigned larger class lists and women professors being provided more limited research funds, the women gathered one day to research every aspect of employment differences. They first measured all the offices in the evening—and discovered men's were more than twice as big. Then they examined salaries and research funding (this was more difficult; they were originally told the information was "unavailable")—men came out way ahead. Then they examined committees that granted funds—very few women on board. There was not a single woman department head; there never had been.

It didn't take a rocket scientist—or any other kind of scientist—to figure out that the inequities were huge. Kudos to MIT, however, because once the facts were presented to them from the well-researched results, they took fast action to remedy the situation on all fronts. Perhaps the unspoken threat of a lawsuit prompted the changes, but salary and grant improvements were made, and fast.

What's the message in this? Discrimination is often so subtle that neither the men nor the women even recognize it as such. If it is mentioned, the usual male answer is, "It's just the way the world works." Perhaps the subtle discrimination has been accepted for many years without question, but not any more. Whatever it takes—tape measures, routing out unpublished salary numbers, a united front, a willingness to challenge the status quo—the world is going to have to adapt to the changing gender and color of the workforce and pay people fairly and by ability, not body parts. Many people feel the determination of the MIT women professors was an inspiration to others, men and women from all cultures, to not accept the conspiracy of silence but to do their homework and challenge the unequal status.

If you're not up to the fight, however, look for smaller companies, women-owned and -run companies (certainly not a guarantee, however), or do a thorough research job on the pay scales in any company you are considering.

You Say Potato, I Say Potahto: Understanding Company Cultures

Countries have unique styles and personalities; so do people, and so do companies. Some people feel a bad "fit" in a company is due to cultural differences—by this we don't mean ethnic or gender differences, but personalities. Companies vary extensively in their personalities, ranging from a high-energy, risk-taking, creative mentality to a middle-of-the-road thinking, to the stuck-in-tradition bureaucratic mentality. Or anything in between. If you understand the culture of the company in which you are interested (and much information can be gleaned from the business press), you will have a giant leap forward knowing if you will fit in successfully.

One way to research this (we know your research skills are extraordinary) is to schedule an information interview with someone in the company or find someone who works there for an informal conversation (there is more on information interviews in Chapter 10). Ask questions that help you understand how the company communicates with all levels of employees, how involved employees are in decision making, what the basics like promotion schedules are, networking, even dress codes. We have one friend who, in her job search, hung out in the cafeteria and started up casual conversations in the parking lot. She learned a great deal about how employees were treated and paid and how the company resolved problems.

Another research tool is to read the company annual reports, brochures, or other company literature, and check into their Web sites. You can gain a great deal of information reading the material and reading between the lines, if possible. Remember, however, that published materials are usually put together by public relations firms, who major in positive spin and lovely verbiage and pretty pictures. The not-so-pretty stuff is harder to dig out.

While you are compiling this information, check it against what you know about yourself. Does the company have a demanding, high-pressure, many-deadline environment requiring quick decision making and flexibility? Are those some of your shining qualities? Will your potential position be stimulating, with fun-loving coworker support, or will you be shuffled into a back room with air conditioners whirring and dust swirling and nary another person in sight? It depends on your personality, doesn't it? What culture fits you best?

There's one more piece of research you may want to consider if you are a working parent: Many companies are becoming far more family-friendly because they have begun to realize employees are more productive if their family concerns are in order. (Hel-l-o-o-o? What took them so long?) IBM has a nanny-resource guide, Bristol-Myers offers a year of baby formula, Chase Manhattan Bank has a back-up child care facility when babysitters don't show and even resources for elder care assessment and support. Others making a "Top Ten" list of progressive companies are Bank of America, Cigna, Deutsche Bank, Fannie Mae, First Tennessee Bank, Eli Lilly, Lincoln Financial Group, Lotus Development, and Prudential Financial Services. (IBM has made this list for 12 years in a row.) *Working Mother* magazine produces a list of the top 100 companies every year, and because this information applies to fathers as well, it might be worth reviewing in your research.

Can We Talk?

Communication is the foundation of all human interaction, as we all know. The differences in male/female communication styles have been thoroughly researched and reported, with results popping out in best-selling books, magazines, and television documentaries about "brain sex," and the information is even making top ten lists on nighttime talk shows. The jokes abound, which helps to lighten tensions. But the bottom line remains the same: As long as both genders continue to define the other by historical roles and stereotypes, without recognizing intellect and achievement or being willing to broaden opportunities, gender roles will not change. And our communication styles will reflect the same old ingrained patterns. Changing a company culture is like trying to shove an elephant, but it can be done, with patience and teamwork.

As you prepare to make the leap from academia to the business world, the first insight you will have is that virtually nothing in the world of communication and hierarchies has changed. Even if you go into a business run by women, "male" language style may still dominate—and it should not be called "male"; it might be better titled "assertive" or "competitive" or "aggressive" or "controlling" because this is the usual business communication pattern. Women are getting adept at presenting a stronger style of talk, easily speaking the language of competition, and this is benefiting the business world as much as it is frustrating those who feel women should be seen and not heard.

But the obvious remains: The world—from government to politics to education to religion to business—is male-developed, male-designed, and male-dominated. Letting others, still occasionally referred to as "women and other minorities," into the higher echelons, remains an unwelcome option. This should not be a surprise to anyone. If you held all the marbles in the game, could create and change the rules at whim, and made buckets of money making big decisions, what incentive would you have to share this power, much less give up any of it?

So, ladies, in spite of your masterful accomplishment of those three initials after your name, you are about to enter a world that is just as male as—or even more so than—the ivory tower you are leaving. We do not mean to imply that the business world is comfortable for all men, either. There are many males, and not just the ones with quiet or introverted personalities, who prefer to simply be left alone to do their job and don't wish to enter into verbal battles for turf, salary, or privilege and who struggle with a macho mentality found in many work environments. This is an individual issue. But we do think extended years in academia tend to infuse doctoral students with the thinking that the only true calling is the life of the mind and that academia environs are somehow far superior to the disrespectful activities of commerce. We encourage you to toss out those restrictions and be smart about the business world before you jump into it.

Minority men often have the same issues to deal with as they contemplate a change of venue from academia to industry. Extra degrees, pages of scholarly writings, a love of teaching and solitary research, and an environment that tends to be supportive of cultural differences often do not prepare graduates for the fast-paced hard give-and-take and lack of political correctness of the real world, especially if the individual is from a culture that teaches one not to challenge the system.

There are many books and articles available for those who are particularly interested in extending their knowledge about communication differences. What we stress is that leaving the academic world for the business world is akin to the cliche of leaping from the frying pan into the fire. The academic world of ultra-political correctness, semester/quarter-driven rhythms, an elitist "life of the mind" philosophy, and mild (or severe) disdain for the rough-and-tumble world of business is like a warm, self-contained soufflé pan filled with ingredients that are narrowly defined, precisely measured, and highly praised. Students know exactly what is expected of them, when, how, and at what time.

The business world, however, is full of fiery energy, with rules that are often made to be ignored or broken, mavericks and free-spirited individuals lurking behind fancy desks in corner offices, ingredients that are tossed and singed and mixed and changed at whim, whose rhythms are completely dictated by the bottom line. It is a very different mind-set; even communication styles take on a different slant.

Jan recently worked with a group of Vietnamese men, all of whom had doctorates in humanities from their own country, who were now working in the computer biotech field. They reported that the language barrier was easily overcome, and work requirements were quickly learned, but understanding the company culture was a huge challenge. These men felt their biggest issue was learning the company communication channels, getting appropriate feedback, and figuring out how decisions and promotions were made. "The dress code was easy," one man laughed, "it's always casual in this business. But we were used to a more relationship-based environment, and it was quite an adjustment." They didn't know to whom to report or who would help them with problems, and they were mystified by the common response—"Find a way to resolve it yourself"—so they tended to stick together to try to figure out solutions on their own. Their work ethic was superb, and in spite of the cultural challenges they were a successful band of software engineers with Ph.D.s in humanities.

The Stepford Workforce

Please don't fall into the trap of believing if we were all just a little bit more alike, with androgynous clothes and same stripes and attitudes and language, we would solve all the problems in the workplace. It just isn't so. Making everyone alike would eliminate all the diverse and wonderful traits that we bring to our lives and working positions. Wouldn't it be frustrating to get up every morning and face a bunch of clones? How boring! It's uniqueness that blossoms in the work environment, diversified talents and individual skills and a wide range of personalities. And, because we're still in the gender/culture chapter, allow us to add another aspect of our individual talents: How do you showcase your talents, ideas, skills, and creative thinking?

For instance, what do you do if you have just thought up a terrific idea to solve a thorny problem? Well, a man would most likely announce his idea to the decision-making powers and claim it loudly and rightfully as his own—as he should. A woman, we're sad to report, often will announce in a meeting, "I'm not sure if this idea would work, but what about . . . ," and poof! Her validity and original idea are instantly discredited; she discredited her own idea herself! Was she sleeping through those assertiveness training classes? She blows away credibility by revealing basic insecurities and using a deflated language style. You would be amazed by how often this happens.

Communication research tells us this is one of the most common ways women undermine their own talents. Five minutes into that same meeting, a man might bring up her same idea in a strong, positive manner, and he's an instant hero. She is slumped in her chair, angry at herself for not claiming the deserved credit. Letting talents and bright ideas show and taking credit for them is the best way—no, the *only* way—to make a significant contribution to a workplace.

So how do you showcase your talents? The best way you know how—by speech, action, responsibility, performance. And don't forget to bring out your sense of humor, the ultimate weapon for defusing sticky situations. It's safest to remember that, as you experienced firsthand in academia, people from differing backgrounds express themselves differently and have different work styles and ethics, and we all need to focus on talents more than temperaments.

One of the reasons this book encourages you to examine your own skills and to determine your own personality style in working, communicating, negotiating, and building new skills is that we authors get panic attacks at the very thought of an androgynous workplace. We break out in hives at the thought of mental uniforms; identical language patterns; same work styles, problem solving, and discussion formats; and even similar hair styles. The words "individuality" and "diversified" may be overused, but they still give a powerful message. If you want a nameless, faceless workforce, don't come to us. Tell it to the Marines.

Let's Hear It for the Zipper

Yes, sexual harassment is real. Yes, it can affect both males and females, but the average is 95% male harassment of females. No, you won't always be listened to, understood, or even guaranteed that you will keep your job if you become a whistle-blower. (We still live with a pattern of shooting the messengers and firing the whistle-blowers regardless of gender.) There are many cases of harassment winding their way through the courts, ranging from well-deserved to downright frivolous, and the legal system is still trying to find a clear, concise description of exactly what constitutes harassment and what does not. A commonly used version of the definition is "unwanted sexual advances, physical or verbal conduct of a sexual nature, or requests for sexual favors made as a condition for employment, [which] creates an offensive or hostile environment, or interferes with work production." Such behavior includes sexual-innuendo jokes, lewd or suggestive comments, touching, or unwelcome gifts.

There are even some highly publicized examples of lawsuits backfiring on the initiators, another form of backlash perhaps. Others are afraid of reporting problems because they know their jobs could disappear. Where does harassment start, and where does it end? Many feel it starts in childhood behavioral patterns and, if not stopped, will continue to grow. It was reported in 1992 that up to 75% of men think women find sexual advances flattering, but 75% of women find them offensive. We have a serious communication problem here.

Harassment shows up in different ways. It can be as subtle as a smirk or as devastating as a rape. It can be in a word, a touch, a threat, a shove. It can come through the mail, over the airways, from the media. And it pervades all cultures, all countries.

The most common kind of harassment found in the workplace is verbal, and that's where an understanding of communication styles becomes necessary. In most of the world, boys are raised with a form of "status" speech, the kind of "King of the Hill" mentality that often shows up in nursery school playgrounds and continues throughout male lives. It is an inner-directed, owner-occupied style that produces the desired independent attitude necessary in warrior cultures.

Most women are taught (let's leave biology out of this for the moment, OK?) to be the supportive gender, thus developing a "connective" style of speech. As Sam Keen wrote in *Fire in the Belly,* women's role in a warrior society is "beauty and duty." That's a subordinate, compassionate, nurturing, and supportive role—and yes, many women thrive under these conditions. Others, however, find the traditional female role too constricting, too devoid of growth opportunities, and look for ways to rebel. What these rebellious women often forget, however, is that they may want to examine their speech style to encompass the more acceptable competitive style, although many women feel this is unnecessary. "We wore their clothes," one woman reported, "invaded their offices, and knocked on their glass ceilings, but we are having a hard time combining our natural connective style of speech with a more assertive style needed in a male-dominated workplace."

Men live comfortably in their physical world, a world in which they have been trained since early childhood. The competitive, winner-take-all, I'm-in-charge mentality, with anger as one of the few emotions allowed, combined with practical joking and put-down humor, makes for a language style that is physical and open. Women, however, tend to be encouraged to live in their emotional world, tuning into a wide range of emotions of their own and of all others around them. Their nurturing, connective, let's-not-hurt-any-feelings mentality encourages a language style that is supportive and subtle. Women can get emotionally hurt by words even when there is no physical action; for men, the old adage "action speaks louder than words" is paramount.

Why are we talking about this? Because in sexual harassment issues, men will say, as we heard one man testify, "I didn't touch her, I didn't hit her, I didn't fire her. So what's the big deal?" But the woman will say, "It's the words he used, the awful words, that frighten me." He's living in a physical world, a world in which action counts most; she's living in an emotional world in which words have potent powers. This is not new stuff, folks, this is as old as our species. But it is coming up more often because our gender roles are becoming blurred and the freedoms to pursue our own career goals are becoming more available.

Meanwhile, the intellectual world is trying to make sense of the whole mess. And that's where we are now. Legal guidelines, business rules and definitions, and bureaucratic bumblings are all involved as we try to sort out the language and steer a safe path to the future.

Our suggestion to women and men is to know that gender and culture differences abound in the real world as much as anywhere else, and these issues are real and painful, but they are resolvable. Suggestions as to how to deal with it include (a) documenting everything if you are in an uncomfortable position, but not smiling and walking away from rough comments; (b) answering back immediately with a firm refusal to tolerate such behavior and reporting all abuses to supervisors immediately; (c) contacting an attorney, if necessary; and (d) your absolute last resort if you get no help from your organization: polishing your résumé and going job hunting. A position that allows or ignores sexual harassment is no place to work.

We can't predict how issues will be resolved, because every case is different. Sometimes the results will parallel those in the academic world: Young people have been kicked out of school for rotten or even semi-rotten (we'll spare you the details) behavior, and people have been "let go" from work for the same behavior. But be aware that it is far more difficult to get rid of an offensive employee than it is an obnoxious student, and many times the zipper will win if it belongs to an exceptionally bright or valued male employee. No, it's not fair, but whoever said life was?

Been There, Done That, Got the T-Shirt

"I was told [by a prestigious women's college] that I was 'aggressively intellectual' and 'extravagantly feminine.' In essence, I was too pretty and too smart. How can you fight that?" This recent graduate was even told by her adviser that the women's college reported to him that they wouldn't pursue her to fill a teaching position because they didn't like the dress she was wearing! "Isn't that astonishing?" she added. Yes, to us it is. We thought women's colleges valued aggressive intellect and didn't give a hoot about style of dress. Apparently this search committee had smaller concerns.

The story has a happy ending, however. This aggressively intellectual and delightfully feminine woman is now a freelance writer publishing in national magazines and working on two impressive manuscripts. Academia missed a live one, but the "real world" will benefit from her brains, talents, and beauty. Her T-shirt ought to read, "I'm having more fun than you are."

Networking

It's Not Only What You Know, But Whom You Know

R emember all the times your parents told you that if you applied yourself to your studies, learned as much   you could, stayed home from the movies with friends to slog through a challenging book for English Lit, and did all your homework, you would be rewarded with a wonderful career with big salaries, bonuses, and a bright future?

They lied.

Well, not completely. They just didn't give you the entire story, probably because they thought you might start skipping school and making Important Contacts that would help you in your unknown future. And you probably would have done just that. Instead, you most likely listened carefully, cruised through high school and college (well, some of you did; others of us had some serious goofing off to do along the way), and even kept right on chugging diligently through a graduate and doctoral program.

Now it is time to reveal the truth: The best way you are going to find a position is by your contacts and connections. The better your connections, the faster you will be hired; with no connections, and no effort to make any, you could be facing a slow, torturous process. And the sad part is that your best contacts may not originate in the academic world. Most areas of academics, particularly the soft sciences and people-oriented fields, simply don't expose students to a broad range of future career options.

"My advisers told me I was selling myself short," reported one new graduate when he announced his decision to leave academia. "And not one faculty member could—or would—suggest contacts for me to pursue. They made it clear I had to rely on my own efforts."

But no one is on their own when they have networking contacts, and we all have far more than we realize. Spin that camera lens to a wide-angle setting and take a good look at all the people you know from your lifetime of personal associations. You have many years of personal and professional network connections, and it's time to focus on them.

Networking is not only for the moment; it is a lifetime activity. We all need to expand and nourish our professional contacts constantly, especially because we never know when a more interesting job may become available. The more people we meet and impress, the more likely we are to find interesting opportunities. Networking takes time and should not be hurried. The purpose is to build solid relationships so that we are remembered and can create the best match between our abilities and the position.

Sometimes, networking is thought of as schmoozing. Whatever the name, the purpose is to exchange information so that you—actually, both people in the relationship—benefit. Many of us consider only the obvious people with whom to network, meaning faculty, past employers, close friends, and family friends. However, any setting in which you are actively involved has contacts. Understand what you are targeting so that you do not waste other people's time. Make a list of potential contacts, people with whom you feel comfortable and can call easily.

Many universities are offering online access to databases with alumni names, addresses, phone numbers, and occupations, and this is a terrific resource. If you have the opportunity to access such valuable information, take advantage. Sometimes, you will need to contact a career counselor at the university for this information; at other times, you will be given the option of going online directly. Naturally, you need an affiliation with the university to tap into its alumni database. Alumni are often most willing to help others when they share a common educational background.

According to many reports from career counseling professionals, about 80% of job opportunities are not advertised. Openings often are filled through promotions, retirements, maternity leaves, the desire to live in certain parts of the world, marriages, and so forth, and the information is typically first discussed within the business. Thus, knowing people inside a company can help you hear about an opening. Networking may be considered a shortcut to finding a job.

Let's widen your camera lens even more to return briefly to our discussion of personalities and then incorporate that information with gender communication styles, because networking is an activity that is most successful when we understand our different ways of interacting.

If you read networking suggestions in magazines or on-line, you will discover that when using the Myers-Briggs Type Indicator language (see Chapter 2), *thinkers* tend to make decisions based on logic, analysis, and objective reasoning and always stay within the rules. *Feelers,* however, tune into their emotional mode for decisions, wanting to make sure they find a fair solution for everyone involved. Accommodation is the only sensitive and satisfying way to resolve issues for feelers.

Most women, with their finely tuned emotional modes, are geared toward consensus and collaboration. As networkers, they value tact, sensitivity, and tuning into work styles and personalities of others. Even the introverted ones seek harmony and mutual decisions.

If you are strong in the thinking mode, you prefer to make decisions based on a power or status position, you will create new rules to solve problems, and you are not interested in whose feelings get hurt along the way. Principles rule; the solution is all, regardless of feelings. The hierarchy is more important than consensus.

What happens next? The thinkers often come across as (or are accused of being) cold, uncaring, and insensitive. Feelers may come across as (or are accused of being) overemotional, hysterical, and offering unnecessary advice. Neither is particularly productive in a networking situation. The thinker goes for status, domination, and control, which not only will torpedo a mutual information-sharing situation fast. The feeler may sacrifice solutions in an attempt to keep everyone happy.

Understanding these personality types should help us work at creating, not destroying, our networking relationships, which not only will benefit us in our job searches but also will be a powerful tool in work environments, even home and community activities. Networking is a lifelong talent, and worth using.

Introverts and Extroverts

We can hear all the introverted readers gasping in fear when they read our urge to "network," for this is probably not an area that is comfortable for them. Shrinking violets may make bland impressions, and this can be a big problem. As the *Wall Street Journal* reports on its Web site (Tullier, 1998), "There simply is no such thing as a job or career field in which you can be rewarded entirely for what you know and how well you work." Being visible by building connections can be painful for shy job seekers and not conducive to the important process of letting others know of your talents, both as a job seeker and when in a growing position.

A Few Simple Rules

1. Understand that you are not bothering people. Most people enjoy talking about themselves and their jobs, especially if they are satisfied with their work.

2. Start small, making one or two new connections a day as you build your confidence and referral list. It gets easier. Really.

3. Asking a question, whether profound or innocuous, is an easy way to break the ice. Once you lurch past the initial gulp and stammer, your natural talents will come through and the conversation will begin to flow easily. Connecting over a shared interest, a current event, or even the weather will work if you let it.

4. Listen! The basic counseling advice of all time: Listen, listen, listen. If you want that conversation to flow easily after you initiate it, you must listen to what people say. Introverts often have sharp listening skills and know that extroverts love to talk, so all the introverts have to do is wind them up and watch them go. We learn a lot more from listening than from talking, as you know (ever try telling that to an extrovert?).

5. If your confidence sags, review your skill list and remind yourself of all the terrific talents you have to offer to the world. A little ego boost goes a long way.

6. Choose your social activities and events, such as cultural, art, or educational seminars, with forethought. Most meetings have a structure and an agenda that allow you to breathe easily and network casually. Skip the ones that tend to make you nervous. You will have plenty of other opportunities to network successfully.

7. You know the "Just Do It" slogan invented by Nike? It applies to many situations, and this is one of them. When you are feeling in one

Networking Ideas

Where do you find ideas for networking? Besides talking to friends, acquaintances, professors, and family contacts, examine the real world for ideas. For instance, when you read the paper, consider the companies and the people you are reading about. How could you make contact with them? Sometimes, even when you do not know the person, you can send an e-mail or a letter and you will receive a reply. What magazines and journals do you read?

Even TV can give us ideas, although we haven't found many particularly stimulating ideas for job openings in the programs labeled "entertainment," unless you would like to rewrite silly commercials, or get rid of all the inane conversations (maybe scriptwriting is in your future after all?). The news, however, regularly reports future-oriented outlooks of occupations and the needs of the population during the next several years. If you miss the details, every local/national news station has a Web site on which you can find the exact words the newscaster read on the screen.

Networking Through Writing

Writing letters instead of making phone calls is sometimes easier for the introvert, and it can be a time-saver for a scattered extrovert. Because many people today send e-mails, a letter may be considered old-fashioned, but it is still in excellent taste and pleasant to receive. Your excellent writing skills make this an easy process.

And you can write. Oh my, how you can write. Your biggest challenge, however, will be to escape the slow-paced, scholarly, fancy-worded style used in academia and make your current letters short and to the point (with one or two sentences for each idea), powerful, and maybe even breezy and light-toned. Your reader will certainly appreciate the brevity.

Networking Through Contacts

Now that you recognize how the real world is different from the academic environment, you may be confused as to how to network with the "outside." Rest assured, outside and the academy may be different worlds, but they share many common threads.

of your uncomfortable, shy, retiring moods and there is
chance to network . . . Just Do It. The time will come when
or long-winded explanations don't cut it. Just do it.

8. Speak up—no matter how hard it is. Some people call this the
and deliver" style, because if you don't take a stand and deliv
message, interests, work goals, or desires, who will?

9. Tongue-tied when someone answers your phone call? You kr
answer to this one—make notes ahead of time, read them ove
calling, and refer to them as needed during the conversatio
keeps you focused, on track, and calms the jittery nerves. A
this is a good trick for all personality types.

As for you extroverts, no list of suggestions is necessary—all you
remember is to make sure your listening skills stay sharply tuned. W
professional collaborators who are extreme in each direction, with irr
extroverts and deep-thinking introverts working well together. Many (
have years of successful and fun-loving collaboration in both perso
professional relationships. An infinite number of good combinations a
sible when the effort is made.

Introverts and extroverts are equally good at networking even
extrovert appears to be more capable of meeting more people. Meetir
ple is only one aspect of networking. What you have to say and how y
it are also important. The extrovert who naturally meets many peop
have to follow through with substance. The introvert will have to rea
to others even when uncomfortable and make connections using his
skills.

You probably know instinctively which way you lean, but you can
the basics in Chapter 2. Recognize your skills and rely on your streng
cover up your less-developed traits. Try role playing or pretending th
are the opposite of yourself. What have you learned? What can you do I
You want to be able to make connections, because networking is imp
for all of us.

Whether you are still in school or actively job seeking, begin netwo
as soon as possible. Persist no matter what the early results may be.
closely with people you know and like because you will be more comfor
Again, prepare for all meetings. Consider different opportunities. Rec
your strengths and constantly remind yourself of them.

Many people say they cannot relate to those academic types; that is simply not the case. Even academics have to function in the outside world. They are involved in their communities and active in politics and local issues, attend religious ceremonies, are involved in sports, and even attend parties at which they may be the only gainfully employed people outside the business world. These people have varied and interesting connections, just as you do—often better connections if they've been around longer. And speaking of connections, don't just focus on your close pals and academic friends. Consider your relatives and family friends as well as neighbors and community associates. Think like an entrepreneur and be creative. Talk to people you do not know; consider every possible source for information, leading to someone who will have a lead on a new beginning.

Every contact you make will help to build up your confidence. Before you know it, you will be reaching out to people you've never met and setting up meetings with them to talk about your future. When they suggest you meet with their friends, people who may not even know your original friends, you know that you have reached the level of networking that leads to all kinds of possibilities.

A viable source of information and way to establish networking contacts is to watch magazines and newspapers like the *Wall Street Journal* for quotations from professors, authors, or established authorities on a variety of topics. You are massaging their egos at this point, but because they do have real-world contacts, are usually extremely articulate, and enjoy sharing information, it's another lead.

Who knows when you will meet the person who will help you land your new job? One friend of ours made a contact that led to a job offer while he was standing in line at a grocery store. Talking to your local banker, someone you see in the hardware store, or even someone sitting next to you in a waiting room could turn out to be helpful. Remember your neighbors if you have good relationships, and you should. Neighborhoods are filled with people from different occupations, and they may have friends in a field of interest to you.

Opportunities are everywhere. Any social possibilities, religious meetings, and community affairs are all possibilities. So are your children's school, their sporting events, volunteer organizations, and, of course, don't forget your fellow students. They know many people outside their academic circle also. You may feel that you are in a cocoon while refining your dissertation, but, in reality, one is always smart to live a well-rounded life and include many different activities.

If you are volunteering your time and energy for a nonprofit organization, a hospital, or a professional organization or coaching a team of 8-year-olds (they have working parents), remember to talk to all those people with whom you have contacts. When you do volunteer work, accept positions that highlight your skills. People are apt to remember and appreciate workers who do their jobs well. One can never be certain of who knows someone in a position to help you.

Writing a list of your activities and matching names of people you have met may lead to a new possibility. Don't be shy about asking these people if they know someone who might be willing or able to help you. At the same time, be somewhat selective. When you seriously network, you want to make sure that you are being recommended by someone you feel can help you. You certainly do not want to be recommended by a dud or someone with a negative personality! Even if you are an introvert, brush up on your limited extroverted skills by forcing yourself to reach out. You'll probably be surprised by how easy it is to make new friends and find out about additional possibilities.

Networking on the Internet

What an exciting new world we have for exploring information, ideas, and networking—the Internet. If you have written a dissertation, you most likely have extensive experience surfing the Net. Answering ads and Internet listings can take longer than personal networking, but one should certainly use all possibilities. Consider the sites you visited, the chat rooms you contacted, the research you conducted, the organizations you kept in touch with, and then, in your ever-so-organized style, make a list of the job sites that might be helpful.

When you get ready to send out networking e-mail, your message would be most effective if you include basic information, such as the business/industry you were researching, the position you were interested in (if you know it), and a comprehensive sentence about your skills and sparkling personality. Short and sweet is always more powerful. You just spent entire chapters defining how great you are; now let the world know!

Appendix C includes a beginning list of sites that we suggest you investigate. Please remember these sites appear and disappear as if zapped by a magic wand, and there are new ones all the time. This list is up-to-date as of this writing, but tomorrow, who knows? Internet savvy is vital, so make it one of your constantly updated skills.

Informational Interviews

These interviews are exactly what their title suggests: You make an appointment for a phone or personal interview to ask questions of someone already working in a field you find interesting. Make a list of questions ahead of time about the aspects that interest you, such as potential and comparable earnings, evaluation processes, company vision or goals, communication styles, the "culture" of the company, opportunity for advancement, or anything else (including "What do you consider the most/least exciting part about working here?"). If you do so, you will find answers and solid information—sometimes more than you bargained for!

Your networking skills are an asset when conducting informational interviews, not just when trying to get to the interview stage for a position. Make sure which type of interview you are having, because you do not want to use an informational interview to ask for a job (although, as you read in Chapter 10 on interviewing, such turnabouts have happened more than we realize.) Be extremely clear about your expectations when you request a meeting. Watch the time and be direct. The type of people you want to meet are typically very busy.

In addition, do not stray from the focus of subject toward information such as job openings. People resent being used, and they have no time for babblers. When they are generous enough to meet with you to discuss an area of expertise or experience, maintain the boundaries. Besides, they know you are probably looking for a job or you would not be meeting with them. Deception during the interviewing process does not say much for your ethics, and the interviewers will not be impressed. If they raise the possibility of a job, fine. But otherwise, avoid the subject, stick with the concept of an informational interview, and find out as much information as you can about them, their experiences, and their suggestions.

At the end of the meeting, summarize the conversation so that you are clear about what was said. Repeat any referred names with the phone numbers and addresses. If you contact any people who were suggested by an interviewer, be sure you have permission to use his or her name. And when you do contact other people, use the referring name right away. Most busy people are more eager to meet with you if you were recommended by a networking colleague.

Steps for Networking

We have discussed networking styles for introverts and extroverts, tied in with gender styles, but there are some other pointers that might be useful to you that we include here.

Remember that networking works both ways. Perhaps you can help the person with whom you are meeting on another issue or at a later day. One does not want to be pushy, but a shy, quiet person will not impress anyone. Use good judgment.

Networking should be well organized to be effective. Just don't think you can call a few people and job openings will be heaped on you. What follows are some strategy ideas.

CONTACTS

1. Make of list of people you know who might be helpful to your career.
2. Make a list of people with whom you come into contact (organizations, etc.).
3. Make a new list of people whom others have suggested to you but whom you do not already know.

People you know are your first target; people with whom you share interests are next. People who are new to you are your third point of interest, and this is where you need to plan ahead so that you are comfortable and confident. That first impression is critical. And never discount coincidence. Indeed, plan on it. When you have the opportunity to meet with someone, take full advantage. You are simply building bridges for now and your future, and there are many places to cross. You may even fall in the water occasionally (to stretch the metaphor slightly) because you burned those bridges during your job search, but dry clothes and a smile will push you onto the right bridges again.

Successful networking breeds continued interest. This is a lifetime activity, and the more you use these opportunities, the more comfortable and interested you will become. Visualize successful encounters. Use detailed analysis. Choose your company, the type of person you would like to meet, think of the office you would like to have. Some people we know even admitted to selecting—mentally—the furniture they would like.

Now that you are comfortable and have found a person with whom to network, what do you want to discuss with her or him? Try to focus your networking around positive people as much as possible. Obviously, you cannot avoid negative contacts, but you will want to limit your time with the down-minded people because they can make you feel unqualified, and who needs that? Positive people send out vibes of energy and encouragement and inspire you to look forward to your next encounter.

Believe it or not, your classmates have lives of their own, too, and friends, families, and contacts you may know nothing about. Talk to them, and share goals and plans. Even though they may have similar skills and abilities, their job interests may differ, or they may have different opinions about what constitutes the ideal job. They may be more than willing to help you.

Professional organizations are wonderful resources because you are meeting with people with similar interests. The *Encyclopedia of Associations* (1999) is a reference book found at many libraries. Check this reference if you are having trouble finding appropriate groups, or check it to make sure you have not left out a group that would be helpful to you. Attending meetings for the first time is easier if you know someone in the group or at least the name of someone in the group.

Do your homework: Call the chairperson before the meeting for that initial contact. Upon arrival, introduce yourself as soon as you can. Meetings usually include time for socialization, giving you the opportunity to meet with many members. You never know when you will meet someone interesting or a perfect contact. Do not try to impress people until you know a bit about them. Once you have a good understanding of their interests, then you can find common ground and make connections and friendships.

Recognize that, throughout your networking, you will encounter gatekeepers. These are people who hold positions of influence and can limit your contacts with the people you want to meet or who can make decisions that affect your job search. Be friendly yet remain focused on your goals. Winning over the gatekeeper may open more doors that you dreamed.

Who is in the power seat? By paying attention to their needs and influences, you will attract their attention. Be positive, make creative suggestions if that is your strength, and show interest in their work. Asking questions is a good way to show interest. You will benefit from hearing their answers as you expand your knowledge and build friendships. Enthusiasm in their work and interests is always appreciated, as long as you do not go overboard and make them feel you are "kissing up" (we cleaned up that expression from the usual ones we've heard).

Network Mentoring

Network mentoring is an effective and necessary tool for many successful people. The term includes peer mentors and traditional mentors. Traditional mentors often start as a role model, develop into a mentor, and eventually become a sponsor. But the traditional approach is not what we always need. What is important is that all of us use our relationships with those colleagues who have additional experience from which we can learn and benefit.

We can learn from many different people because we have different perspectives. Mentoring typically suggests that we give support and information, increasing with each success. Mentoring may be considered advice informed by experience. As one foundation administrator observed, "It's by intuition based on my interpretation of the person and I don't see that every person needs the same type of mentoring." The process of network mentoring is important because we both exchange beneficial information.

Mentoring means improving the abilities of the future of the protégé. But who is the protégé? You and your mentoring partner can both benefit. Recognize your abilities as well as your mentor, bounce ideas back and forth, and watch the progress you both make in your careers. A true mentor senses accomplishment when his or her protégé develops abilities and the mentor has provided insights to help that person, as a businesswoman said:

> My role is not to guide them in a specific direction, but to give them general counsel about the qualities of mine and experience and the competencies that they need so that they can take advantage of opportunities so that they can create their own future.

Time and respect are necessary to develop a relationship: "You need to care about the person," observed a woman partner in an accounting firm.

Reevaluate your mentoring relationships. When your mentor is helping you, you will be aware of the benefits. When someone states that they want to mentor you, make sure the relationship is advancing. Sometimes, people like the idea of having a protégé around for their skills but they fail to help advance a career. When you fail to get your mentor's attention, when you notice jealousy, or when your mentor has no time for you, recognize the signals that the time has come for you to move on. There are always other people willing to be mentors. Therefore, find ones who may not always be in the most powerful position, but rather ones who have the time and energy and the interest in you.

Consider the friends you contact regularly, and make yourself available to mentor and be mentored. Become a good listener. Reflect on what you are hearing, clarify by repeating statements so that your interpretation is correct, and then carefully give an opinion if one is sought. A good mentor offers further opportunities to mentor others, be mentored, and, consequently, advance one's own skills. Always remember that negative feedback can be equally important and accept that advice gracefully. The process of mentoring is long term and, if effective, can last a lifetime. Avoid the "me first" attitude and remember that giving begets receiving. A successful mentoring relationship is mutually rewarding. Now is the time to recognize that you need others' help just as they will appreciate your help at another time.

Many successful people appreciate informal mentoring. The relaxed structure is typically more effective than structured or arranged mentoring because the relationship happens naturally. With appreciation of each other, both parties benefit. "I was not aware of the mentoring relationship for many years because everything was so subtle and natural." This businesswoman now appreciates all their time together and looks back and recognizes the advantages she had because she was mentored.

Mentoring is an evolution, a need to counsel, listen, and trust. "Sometimes I just listen," one researcher reported. Don't rush these special relationships. Begin early to develop friendships when you recognize a special connection. Finding common interests enables a relationship to develop meaningfully. Building on commonalities can open ideas, and additional common concerns can be found. Help goes both ways, and we never know when an opportunity will come along because of the influence of another person.

Sometimes, the hidden values appear when we least expect them. As one woman reported, "I feel as though I get a lot more than I give in terms of relationships. There are usually things that come back in an intangible way."

"I don't see mentoring in a career situation to be much different from raising children," said a professional responsible for many employees.

Do you have a mentor? What characteristics does he or she have that you especially appreciated? What characteristics did your mentor not have and that you wished for? Remember, we can have more than one mentor. Network mentoring means that we have many mentors and that we mentor many others. We are never so old or so far in our careers that we should stop developing mentoring relationships.

---

1. What are the qualities you admire in others?
2. Who might make a good mentor?
3. Examine your list of skills.
4. Think of whom you might be able to help.
5. Write thank-you notes.
6. Stay in touch.

Here, we set out six things to think about as you consider creating or entering into a mentoring relationship.

To sum up network mentoring, this following super-short list may become the most valuable to you, especially when you officially enter the world of commerce with its inherent politics, wide variety of coworker personalities, and unique opportunities to be, and become, a good mentor.

BECOMING A GOOD MENTOR

Listen.
Reflect.
Focus.
Respond, be polite.
Cardinal rule: Try not to offend anyone.

A quick review of mentoring and networking includes several thoughts. First, never restrict the number of mentors you may have. Multiple mentors are an asset. Second, recognize that mentoring works in two ways so that both parties benefit. Third, do not feel that mentoring occurs on the same level. Another person below your position, above your position, and at the same level all offer valuable insights into problems. Use everyone's skills and think nonhierarchically. Fourth, remember that these relationships may last a lifetime. Never think of the relationship as ending, because you never know when you will need someone's advice or when he or she will ask for your words of wisdom. You always want to be aware of others in the business world and consider any opportunity to add to your circle of networking mentors.

Networking offers a world of opportunities. Take advantage of every opportunity, no matter how inconsequential it may appear at the time. Continue to meet people, to discover commonality, and to offer support to others.

When you strive to meet someone in hopes of networking, you may get one of several responses: Silence, pleasantness, enthusiasm, or rejection. Timing is everything. If the first opportunity is lost, a superior one is around the corner.

There is one more area on which to aim your close-focused lens, and that is translating the work you have completed in graduate school into topics and talents applicable to a future position. As you get ready to prepare your official résumé in the next chapter, you might want to think about these items.

Many professionals feel that networking is the most valuable single resource for finding new or different career positions. No matter what your

---

Consider the following:

1. During my doctoral career, I have focused on _____.
2. I taught the following classes: _____.
3. I worked for _____.
4. I volunteered _____ times a month for the _____ organization.
5. Some of my interests include _____.
6. I am especially interested in _____.
7. I currently am looking for a position in _____.

---

personality portrait offers, or what inhibitions or exhibitions you lean toward, you will have to extend yourself to communicate your needs and desires to as many people as possible. Short of standing on a street corner with a sign proclaiming, "Have Ph.D., Will Travel," we suggest you use every lens and type of film available to get a clear picture of what opportunities are available, where you feel you would make the best contribution, and who might help you reach your goal.

References

Encyclopedia of Associations. (1999). Detroit, MI: Gale Research.

Tullier, L. Michelle. (1998). *Networking for everyone.* Indianapolis, IN: Jist Works, Inc.

CHAPTER 9

Writing Effective Résumés and Cover Letters

"Why Bother With a Résumé? Just Let Me Talk to Them, They'll Love Me."

So spake an enthusiastic new doc and job seeker, not stopping to consider that he would not even get near a potential job opening without a professional résumé having first winged its way across the company threshold, landing squarely on the desk of the hiring manager.

What's the point of a résumé? Why bother?

Many reasons: Your résumé is a marketing tool, a sales pitch, an attention-getter, and the most effective first step you can take toward finding the job of your dreams. Many people in academia cling to the curriculum vitae (CV) format either because that's all they know or because they feel it's a more powerful tool. A CV is required for academia, but it is not appropriate for the rest of the world. Why not? Because they generally tend to be too long and too focused on papers published, projects completed, classes taught, and presentations given than on the skills used. They also may focus on the theoretical rather than the practical.

A concise, well-phrased résumé, however, focuses on your talents, working skills, and the proven accomplishments that relate to the business world. It is doubtful that anyone will ask you the minute details about your classes or even your GPA; it is definite that you will be asked what unique talents and skills you can bring to particular work requirements. It's the "what can you do for me?" philosophy, and rightly so, because the company will be paying for your time and production.

Advice on how to create a powerful résumé is rampant; any bookstore has shelves of ancient and semicurrent standards, but we've never found one addressing your unique situation of turning academic skills into real-world opportunities. In addition, your computer program has at least one, and perhaps several, résumé templates offering you the option of simply plugging in your wondrous deeds and letting them put it into the proper format. If you choose to go this route, being either busy, or lazy, or hungry for work (or just plain hungry), fine. Skip this chapter. But if you want to create a powerful, professional representation of your talents and accomplishments, stick with us a little longer.

We suggest you build the important information first, and then get to the details about paper, "air," fonts, fluff, and professional appearance. And that's exactly the way we present this information, from the Most Important Stuff (name, format, objective, title, summary, experience, and accomplishments), to the Sort-of-Important Stuff (fonts, paper, bold print, underlines), down to the Not-so-Important Stuff (margins, small details).

The Most Important Stuff

Name

Obviously, the first item to include is your name, address, phone number, fax, and e-mail. You need to be reached. One caveat: For women who are posting résumés on the Internet and are not sure if the site is secure, you are perfectly within your rights to list only a first initial and no detailed personal information—just put an e-mail address or list a voice mail number or answering service so you can be found. After all, jobs are supposed to be nongendered, right? Men can also do this, of course, but as a rule they don't seem to be bothered by having personal information like addresses or phone numbers floating in earthly ethers.

Format

Your next decision in the Most Important Stuff concerns the format and how you will list your accomplishments. The current acceptable pattern is to keep the résumé to one page, and never more than two. (Wouldn't our academic pals be floored to have to cram their publications into two pages? Publications is the only accepted area you can put on an extra page or two; otherwise, stick to two pages.) If you feel you can't sell yourself and your talents on one page, fine. Use two. But no more.

Your second critical format decision concerns the type of résumé: chronological or functional? It's entirely up to you, depending on your experience, your skills, and your goals. There is a difference.

Chronological. This is the most widely used format. It begins with the most recent information about your employment and responsibilities, and then works backward in time. Many people only go back 10 years, but there are exceptions to this:

1. You aren't old enough to have been in the workforce 10 years.

2. Your most recent position isn't one you are interested in repeating, so you wish to focus on an earlier job you held 15 years ago.

3. You have an exotic array of part-time positions and need to go back in time to show off a particularly responsible position.

4. You took 2 years off to walk across the country (called research, of course) and thus have a huge gap in your work history that needs to be explained somehow.

The chronological is an excellent way to show off your mental growth and increasingly responsible positions, assuming this is the case; it also is a way to showcase the name of a prestigious employer or a particular talent you have developed.

Functional. This format may be uniquely tailored to the recent graduate, because it focuses not on past/current employers and positions but on your specific qualifications for the posted job. It is considered by many who wish to change careers; thus, it would be worth thinking about, because you may be changing from a wished-for academic career into a hoped-for industrial career. The functional format is also widely used by those exiting the military and entering the civilian workforce; you might think of your own experience as similar to this, complete with guns and roses.

A functional résumé lists achievements and skills by—you guessed it—their functions. For instance, you might list three of your general areas of expertise, such as (a) Interpersonal Communication Skills, both written and oral; (b) Organization Skills; and (c) Training Experience, expanding on each with the usual active verbs (listed in Chapter 2). Or you may wish to focus on analytical or research talents, listing three or four specific areas in which you shine, again with major accomplishments.

The good news is that dates are not included on a functional résumé, so you don't have to give away any sensitive information (like the fact that you were the oldest and most silver-haired member of the graduating doctoral class or perhaps that you are still of high school age but brilliant beyond mortal understanding). The bad news is that a functional résumé is not nearly as flexible as a chronological and may limit you if a wide search is your goal. Different talents are needed for different positions, and you may get pigeonholed into one area in which all positions are filled, when in reality you could work brilliantly in five or seven different departments. Also, many hiring managers report functionals are tough for them because they can't evaluate the person's career progress, which is an important chunk of information to most of those in the hiring business. Some folks are being creative and trying to combine the two approaches, which is confusing to us and (we've been told) to the hiring managers, so our suggestion is to pick one or the other and stick with a traditional format. Of course, you may ignore this advice, but please think and plan carefully about which format you select.

If you choose a functional résumé, there is enough information here to get you started, and a stroll through your local bookstore will give you books with ideas of what areas to include or exclude. These are so individual it is difficult to give particulars.

Objective

The first sentence most people put on a résumé is an objective, announcing what kind of job they are seeking. We find two problems with this: first, it may limit you to one small area, when in reality you could be placed in one of several areas of a work environment, and second, everyone knows you're looking for a job just by sending out the résumé, why be redundant? We've seen innocuous statements like, "My objective is to find a position that improves my skills and allows me to advance professionally." Well, isn't that just dandy? The job seeker gets all the benefits. What about the employer? What does the prospective company get from this narcissistic approach? It's wasted space and a quick turnoff. One of our favorite leads was, "My objective is to find a position that best uses my talents so I can help the company grow." As the hiring manager responded, "Well, I still know nothing about this candidate, her talents, or what she has to offer this company. What does she do? How can she help us?" Be efficient: Skip the objective (that line may save precious space) and go straight to a summary statement that shows off your abilities and reaches out to grab the interest of the interviewer/hiring manager and force him or her to keep reading.

Title

Now that you have your name and how others can reach you, have you thought of a suitable title? It isn't critical, but it does help a potential interviewer/hiring manager zoom in on your skill set, and it is mandatory for your own knowledge when doing an Internet search. Forced-choice format on the Internet, remember those?

Do you or did you have a job title? Use it. And, if need be, make it sound important. If a homemaker can call herself a domestic engineer, and a garbage collector is a sanitation engineer, there is no reason why you shouldn't have a title that sounds important and conveys multiple talents. If you were a file clerk in the admissions office, you obviously wish to broaden your career opportunities, so perhaps you could refer to your position as Office Administration Assistant, or as one young man stated tongue-in-cheek, Clean-up Artist. If you typed lab reports for a professor, you could now be a Word Processor, because you obviously know your way around a computer program. If you were or are a sales clerk, you're in Customer Relations; if you repaired anything, you can be a Technician. If you consider yourself a consultant, say so. A trainer? Say so. If you're a wizard computer programmer, we're told you can list yourself as a Software Engineer, but this one makes us a little nervous. You could be a developer, consultant, adviser, coach, trainer, teacher, or instructor. Or a director, manager, interpreter, decision maker, or performer. Just make sure of two things: that it accurately describes your position(s), and it meets your future job goals.

Be wary of titles, however—they can backfire. You'll notice, if you skim résumé books, that many of them don't put a title but almost always put an objective. Because we don't happen to like an objective—redundant, how many professors wrote that on our papers?—we lean toward a comprehensive title. If in doubt, however, leave it out.

Before we forget, put the word *scanner* into your mind-set—scanners seem to like titles as well as other pertinent information. Many large companies are increasingly using electronic scanners to sort résumés, which means they are programmed to search for particular buzzwords of their profession. We suggest that rather than be digitally dumped from the résumé pool, you simply use appropriate words that fit each arena, and put these words in your summary statement.

If you are unsure of the words, look on the Internet searches under different professions, and they'll spit out buzzwords that will make your head spin. Some books recommend you parade these words across the top of the résumé, some even put a nifty box around the words. (We lean toward the traditional look, but it's your call.) If a company requests certain buzzwords, however, get them in somewhere. Companies are trying to match your skills to their required job positions, so make sure the words reflect this. Some of these scanners even rank surviving résumés in order of skill sets and then spit out that ranking to the hiring manager. You might as well be as close to the top of the heap as possible.

Professional Summary

So what comes after your title, assuming you have one? We feel the most professional approach (and most books will tell you the same thing) is to write a powerful Life Summary statement at the top of your résumé. Three short, well-packed sentences summing up your entire life will do nicely. Obviously, this is not easy, especially for those of us skilled in the art of academic jargon. This Summary of Qualifications (call it what you wish: Executive Summary, Professional Summary, Summary of Qualifications, or—our favorite—just plain Summary) must tell as much about you as possible in the fewest possible words. Use phrases, and never use the word "I."

A summary may well be your most difficult résumé writing assignment, but it also is your chance to be the most creative. This is the time to paint the big picture of who you are and what you offer, so word this carefully. No, word this *perfectly*. Every single word counts. If your résumé gets scanned, this is where you'll stay alive and not have your future short-circuited by an electronic wizard who lives by the "Do Not Pass Go" mentality.

The summary sentences can be placed in whatever order tickles your word-smithing fancy, but each one has a direct purpose:

1. It offers a *brief* summary of your extensive experience.

2. It mentions where you received that experience, including any work adventures inside as well as outside the academic realm.

3. It shares the shining attributes of your personality.

And because you are already trying to figure out how to make this summary statement longer (yes, we know you academic types), the answer is yes—if you must, then make it longer, but not much. The main point is to sell yourself in the shortest format possible. Add an appropriate quote if you wish, if you are particularly brave-hearted, but please focus on your skills. And we still think three tight, powerful sentences make the best impression. The attributes may be mixed, such as "dependable, conscientious research assistant," "creative writer dedicated to clarity and understanding," or some such wording, but include all three elements.

Some people feel you should tailor your résumé for specific positions, thus requiring you to "tweak" the summary to focus on particular talents required for each job opening. If you are applying to a variety of positions, this may indeed be necessary, and that's fine if you have no other life—nothing left to do but admire the newly framed doctoral diploma on your wall as you type out 15 varied résumés for 15 various venues. But at this point, wouldn't you rather have one résumé that is so smashing, so powerful, so complete, it could go almost anyplace? Being a job-seeker is tough enough without remembering which of your 15 different résumés goes to what company.

Sometimes, it helps to think of a résumé as a newspaper article, with the "who, what, when, where, why" information appearing immediately. In newspapers, this critical information is usually squeezed into the first paragraph. The details then emerge as the article progresses, with the information lessening in importance as the article winds down to the bottom line. Newspaper editors, being space-conscious, often do their cutting or editing from the bottom up when they know the essentials are in place. Ditto with your résumé; the least important data will be on the second page toward the bottom. (Many business résumé templates list the "Education" credits at the bottom of the second and final page—a bit discouraging after all your academic struggles, eh? But it's still OK to put your degrees earlier, if you have a hang-up about this or if the particular position you are seeking requires this information.)

Because *Who You Are* is the most important information of all, your Sensational Summary Statement, which is the first paragraph, deserves your undivided attention. What follows are some disguised examples of powerful summary statements we have encountered. (All individuals have had some form of work experience before or during their doctoral pursuits; we're assuming you have similar histories. If you have never held a job in your life, this will be a harder assignment for you, and you obviously will focus on your superb talents and skills, untested though they may be.)

> "Over 5 years' experience in progressively responsible positions within the Financial Aid office at the University of Wisdom, resolving unique and challenging problems with an ethnically diverse student body. Excellent interpersonal communication and conflict resolution skills, known for finding innovative and long-term strategies within a structured format. Recognized for strong team-oriented, organizational, and problem-solving abilities."

This example shows a variety of skills that would enhance any business setting. The final sentence here is brief, but could be expanded to include personality traits. As some employers have stated publicly, "Give me a personality that is open to learning, is creative and curious, and I can teach or improve the skill base. It's the *personality* that captures my interest." Or, as the motto states, Hire for personality, train for skills.

If you know you are seeking a position within an organization that advertises for adaptable personality, put that information up front, as shown in the following example:

> "Creative, energetic, responsible individual who works well in both team and individual environments. Strong abilities in researching, analyzing, synthesizing, and interpreting large amounts of data and then presenting it in a workable format. Over 8 years' part-time experience in research division of a large technology corporation."

One woman we know financed her graduate education as a cocktail waitress in a seaside restaurant. (This is not an unusual scenario.) How did she word her summary statement? Positively, of course:

> "Unique talents in resolving unusual, varied, and sometimes difficult requests from a diverse population in a resort community. Exceptional communication skills, along with pleasing personality and a strong desire to help others, resulted in 5 years of increasingly challenging assignments, a permanent training position, and promotion to manager. Seeking a full-time position in Human Resources or related personnel environment."

One fellow was trained as a registered nurse and worked weekends during his doctoral program, using the nursing responsibilities as fuel for his summary statement:

> "Experienced in handling the unexpected: soothing frightened patients leery of a male nurse; proving to skeptical female staff nurses that I was equally capable in all areas of nursing; and reassuring administrative staff that my abilities to gather and interpret diverse data by communication and close observation (finely tuned in my doctoral dissertation) were skills conducive to my goal of a position in hospital administration. Inquisitive, flexible, exceptionally compassionate individual."

For those of you pursuing a position in technology, a summary that includes your technical skills is, of course, the best approach. You will want to specify in the "skill sentence" which systems in which you are literate, such as UNISYS, LOTUS, SDS, UNIVAC, UNIX, Windows 98, PowerPoint, DOS, WordPerfect, Word, mainframes, ABC, and PQRST. (We may be able to get away with being flippant—our editors expect that of us—but please don't try it in a résumé because the reader will know you are fudging facts. Hardly a trustworthy beginning for your budding business career.)

In this situation, if you're so amazingly computer literate that it takes three lines just to show off your talents, save the bulk of the fancy lingo for later in the résumé under a newly created section entitled "Hardware/Software Experience." Simply report in the summary that you are experienced in database management and programming, or whatever appropriate buzzwords fit your skills. (Think "scanner" at all times.) Also, please know that computer skills are paramount for almost any position in today's business community. If you are rusty in everything except word processing, we suggest you use this "down" time, or job search time, to take basic courses or improve current skills. It may be a survival tool.

One field that seems to attract many graduates in the social sciences is that of public relations or media representatives for corporations or ad agencies. These are fields that demand strong people skills, an ability to juggle a multitude of details and projects at the same time, and the talent to keep smiling when you'd rather be tossing recalcitrant clients out the window. If you've never worked in this area and can scare up an internship for a few months for practice, your doctoral degree in any related field—psychology, sociology, even anthropology or other people-oriented specialties—might read like this:

> "Experienced in developing multimedia projects, giving professional presentations, and training personnel for public appearances within both the academic and business communities. Exceptional people/communication skills, recognized for analytical and creative approaches within a variety of situations. Strong writing and public speaking abilities with whimsical sense of humor that has been known to defuse difficult situations."

You get the point by now: three sentences, each with a purpose, in whatever order you feel best represents you and where you want to go.

Accomplishments/Achievements

These are the important details. List your most impressive accomplishments and include not only being in the workforce but community and school involvement, whether paid or volunteer. Each of these accomplishments must support your goals in the position or arena you are searching.

In case you are fuzzy about what particular work environment skills and buzzwords are required, look in the *Dictionary of Occupational Titles*—remember that from your undergraduate classes? It's still a great resource for job descriptions. Of course, the Internet is also a handy resource, as are the many job search sites listed in Appendix C.

For example, if you are applying to a position in which written skills are required, you are a proven commodity with a doctorate to your credit, so highlight your extensive written experiences. If analytical or research skills are required, again you are golden—that's what you've been doing all these years! If supervisory skills are mentioned, surely you have taught classes or supervised small or large groups in your lifetime. In other words, match your accomplishments to the stated requirements.

Here's an example of a recent English Lit graduate seeking a position as editor in the publishing world. The position was listed on a Web site at a small but busy publishing house needing an editor with experience in writing, knowledge of the different genres, and strong communication skills.

The first thing you notice about this is the doctoral degree after Julia's name, so she doesn't have to keep pounding on that topic—it speaks volumes

JULIA SMART, Ph.D.

1234 Main Street
Akron, Ohio 44300

phone: 123.456.7890   email: jsmart@whereever

SUMMARY

Professional wordsmith dedicated to helping others craft exciting ideas into articulate and imaginative prose. Extensive knowledge of literary styles, experienced in encouraging others to create their own style and "voice." Independent, creative, with excellent interpersonal communication skills and extraordinary patience.

PROFESSIONAL EXPERIENCE

UNIVERSITY OF SMART PEOPLE, Akron, OH   **1993-1999**
Director, University Writing Center

Assisted students and staff at all university levels in brainstorming ideas, researching appropriate techniques, and preparing papers of any length or topic.

- Taught classes on research techniques.
- Created software program enabling clients to work independently.
- Prepared extensive lists of easily read materials.
- Wrote Writing Skills manual for Writing Center that resulted in a 50% increase (according to professors) of improved term papers.
- Conducted monthly seminars to assist others in exploring and understanding the various genres outside academics, primarily fiction and nonfiction.

AKRON CITY SCHOOLS,   **1995-1997**
Assistant Writing Coach, Tutoring Center
Coordinated student needs with tutoring counselors

- Evaluated individual writing abilities and experience.
- Matched students with appropriate advisers.
- Conducted follow-up sessions with each student.
- Initiated Creative Writing Seminars for all grade levels.

COMMUNITY ACTIVITIES

FREELANCE NEWSLETTER EDITOR　　　　　　**1990-1995**

Worked with seven community volunteer organizations assisting with newsletter layout, writing, and editing requirements.

- Planned articles for current and future publications.
- Coordinated materials of freelance writers.
- Prepared advertising layouts.
- Edited all written material to fit space and topic requirements.

EDUCATION

Ph.D., English, University of Knowledge
M.A., English Literature, University of Wisdom
B.A., Journalism, University of Acumen

COMPUTER SKILLS

Microsoft Word, WordPerfect; Windows 95, 98, 2000

in three little letters at the top of the page, and that's exactly what you want it to do. Also, the reader knows the education details will be on the second page.

Julia does have her full name, but when posting on the Internet on a site where she wasn't sure about security (in spite of the little locked key diagram in the lower left-hand corner), she simply used her first initial. This is obviously an abbreviated résumé, but you can see a summary statement and how her achievements are listed. Those active verbs that follow each bullet are powerful little critters, and they can be spiced up in any way you wish to get the point across that she is well qualified for this position. This résumé did get Julia an interview, which was the whole point. Last we heard, she was in salary negotiations—but that comes later in the book.

Notice also that there are no dates except her work history—no dates on education degrees, particularly. Broadcasting your age is not considered good form, and it is illegal for anyone in the hiring business to ask you how old you are. (Although they will ask for date of birth on an application form— sneaky, huh?)

Also, no need to say you will supply references on request—that's decidedly old-fashioned, and they already assume that. We're told no one asks for references, or calls the persons on the list, before an interview. Hiring tends to be a linear process, and seldom do people venture out of the established boxes. However, you may wish to add at the bottom of the second page that you are willing to relocate if you know that is a priority and it's OK or desirable with you. In fact, we've seen that information tucked into a summary sentence to announce their mobility right up front, and if moving is a requirement, your availability may launch you to leader of the application pack. If this is the case, write down (on a private notepad) relocation expenses as one of your future salary negotiation issues.

We suggest you either buy, borrow, or simply browse through one of the many résumé books on the market (we happen to be particularly impressed with Martin Yate's series, but to each his or her own taste) to get ideas of the many clever and slightly varied ways you can structure your own résumé.

The Sort-of-Important Stuff

This section is much shorter, because it deals with font and paper selection, bold print, underlines, and italic usage. Here's the scoop.

Fonts

Keep it simple and easy to read. You have no idea how old or challenged are the eyes of the reader, and you don't want to antagonize anyone. Stick with the basics—Times New Roman, Helvetica, Ariel, Courier, or anything in your computer that is clean-cut and easy to read.

And because you're being considerate of eyes, please don't go smaller than a 10-point font. It's best to stay with 12 (which will vary a tiny bit with each font, but be within the general range) and make your readers happy.

Paper

Most human resource folks clearly prefer good white bond paper. Some applicants claim anything on heavy, expensive paper gets a first read, but we are skeptical about that advice as well as the source. A light tan or ivory tone is also acceptable, providing you have matching or similar large envelopes. Yes, the world is electronic, and you may e-mail or fax résumés, but it's smart to follow up with a perfect hard copy by snail mail. And you need large envelopes because you don't ever want to fold, staple, tape, mutilate, clip, or abuse those two precious résumé pages.

Also, skip any creative graphics, fancy borders, cutesy cartoons, or balloons soaring high like you plan to do in your job. Unless you are applying for a position in graphic arts/design, where any creativity is acceptable, your goal is a plain but effective professional presentation.

Have you wandered into one of the proliferating discount office supply megamarts lately? There are so many paper choices you may feel overwhelmed, so just grab the nearest package of what suits your taste, color (but only white or tan/ivory), and budget. Chances are you'll be sending out more than just a few, so more is better.

Bold Print

Advice is mixed here: We like bold print, but only for your name at the top, title if you have one, the word Summary and Professional Experience, and the name of company/organization and your title in that position. Do what tickles your fancy, but please be aware that bold type has been known to throw off scanners, in spite of claims from large companies that their scanners are too sophisticated for such picky nonsense. Why take that chance, especially if you are applying to large organizations that surely use scanners? Use bold sparingly but effectively.

Underlines and Italics

Scanners don't always like underlining, most readers don't like underlining. Neither do we. Nor do we advise you to use italics, not only because we don't like the look, but also because—again—you need to beware of sensitive scanners. Keep both pages clean and neat—no sense in glitzing them up with fuzzy print.

The Not-So-Important Stuff

Now we're down to the real nitty-gritty details.

Margins

The best advice is to aim for "manuscript margins" of 1 inch on all four sides. But if you have enormous vital information to squeeze onto two pages, you can push out the side 1-inch rules here a little if you can't fit all your illustrious career onto two pages.

Also, the justifications you choose for the right side (we're assuming you know to have the left side lined up perfectly) are entirely dictated by your obsessive-compulsive nature, or lack thereof. We've seen squared-off right-hand justifications and frazzled right-hand justifications, and we have no opinion on which is best.

Air

Journalists have a term called *air,* which is any clean, empty space on pages. Anytime you can provide some air, you not only give the reader a break, but you also allow the eye to zero in on certain areas they may wish to reread or discuss with you in the interview. Tightly packed text, as you well know from academia, is hard on the eyes and far too easily ignored. Give them some air. No pictures, no art work, no photos—just air.

So, what's left to put on your résumé? By now we have listed several sites of employment/volunteer/internship/fellowship achievements (never letting one carry over from the bottom of the first page to the beginning of the second page, of course—keep sites and achievements in clumps on a page) but you still need to add a couple of things.

As you noticed on Julia Smart's résumé, she finished off with her education and computer skills, and she centered the text. This is a common format you will see in many résumé books, and one we also happen to like from a visual standpoint. However, if this offends your sensibilities or eyes, you certainly may line every major heading up on the left side of the paper and run them all down like water rushing from a garden hose.

Cover Letters

There is serious disagreement about the necessity of a cover letter, but, in spite of the human resources managers who insist they tear off cover letters and pitch them in the closest wastebasket without a glance, we do recommend you put one together anyway and plan to use it. If a hiring manager or supervisor in your potential department—whose name to whom you addressed the letter because you did your homework—gets the big envelope, chances are that he or she will at least glance at the letter.

So what are the rules? Short. Short. Short. This is your chance to make a smooth introduction and show off your writing skills and good manners. This is also a good time to let some light-heartedness slip into your correspondence, offering a nice balance to a formal résumé.

You will want to continue a professional appearance, so we suggest you either have official letterhead stationery, which you use for both the first page of the résumé and the cover letter, or match the letterhead format by computer. Either one is fine, but having your name and address match is a minor but impressive touch.

Think of your cover letter as three basic paragraphs: Hello, Tooting My Horn, and 'Til We Meet Again. (In current lingo, it might be: Yo, Ain't I Great, and Later, Dude.) Whatever your generation or linguistic preference for thinking about the organization, the actual letter does need to be professional.

Some consultants suggest a cover letter formula of SSSPP: keep it Short, Simple, Spelled correctly, Position-specific, and Positive. Because you are in charge, you would not close with "I look forward to hearing from you" but would write, "I'll call you next week to see if there's anything else you need" or "I'll be in touch soon to set up a meeting time."

Begin by stating where you learned of this position—magazine, newspaper, Internet Web site, career search site, personal reference, or maybe even someone who was standing in line at the post office who said, "Hey, my brother-in-law works at so-and-so company, and he said they were hiring, call him." Skip the post office part, but use a referral name whenever possible, and keep it to a one-sentence opening.

"John Smith suggested I contact you regarding your available position in Marketing." Or, "Judy Jones, one of your sales assistants, felt my outgoing personality and strong communication skills would fit well into your company sales force, and, after researching your organization and product, I agree with her."

If you are answering an advertisement, you need to tell exactly where you read about the open position, including date of publication, and then go on with a comment about how well you fit their profile.

If, however, you are writing cold, with no referral or source to guide you, you'll need a more formal version of the opening line, such as "My interest in your company led to this letter in the hope that you are looking for a person with my particular skills and immediate availability." We've seen cover letters with an unusual twist, such as, "Are you looking for a dedicated, energetic marketing representative with a flexible schedule and proven track record?" Asking a question at the beginning of a letter often begs the reader to keep reading, which is exactly what you want, so you go on in the second paragraph to toot your horn.

The second paragraph (Tooting My Horn, or Ain't I Great) will be to sell your skills. In case you have forgotten what they are, return to your now-completed résumé and pluck a few key points from the achievements lists, making sure the list you include matched the company needs. It's best not to simply restate your achievements—redundancy again—but tighten the wording to reflect how you can make a solid contribution to this company. Also, no dates or places. Just the facts.

The sign-off ('Til We Meet Again or Later, Dude) is important also, because you don't want to leave the response entirely in their hands. We all know how busy schedules will prevent quick responses, from those in academia as well as in the business world. If you leave it up to them, you may wait for months. Take charge—it's your future. Thank the person for his or her consideration, then take the responsibility for follow-up and include a comment that you will contact the person on a certain date—say a week or ten days from now—to see if a meeting or interview can be arranged.

You have now written a short—barely three paragraphs, and short ones at that—cover letter, which is your introduction. Place it on top of your résumé (no staples, paper clips, rubber bands, or Scotch tape, of course, and don't fold or mutilate it either) and mail the puppy off.

Just one final caveat—make sure the cover letter is addressed to the same name that you placed on the big envelope. Too many stories have floated around about Company A getting a letter meant for Company Q, and the bosses even knew each other. This kind of laugh is at your expense. "Oh, but I'd never do that," you insist. Maybe not. But people do, and have done that, and some of them even have doctorates. So it doesn't seem like a silly idea to mention it.

There is one more unusual format you may want to consider, especially if you have seen, in an advertisement or on the Internet, a list of specific qualifications. In this case, many responders have written cover letters with their middle paragraph—the Tooting Your Own Horn paragraph—in two columns. The column on the left lists the company's requirements, and the column on the right matches your skills in the same order. It's effective, easy on the eyes, and direct. And it is certainly worth a try if your skill set is a solid match with what is needed. Although some interviewers tell us they don't like this format, we've heard so many positive responses we think it's valuable to consider. Because you don't know how a potential interviewer will respond, you'll need to make this decision on your own. We like it.

For example, say a position was advertised for a sales representative with specific talents in oral and written communication skills and knowledge of marketing techniques. You might match these to your talents with the second paragraph of your cover letter stating the type of experience you have, set in two columns, shown in the following:

Company Needs	Personal Experience
Oral communication skills	Have extensive public speaking/presentation experience with both individuals and large groups
Written communication skills	Over 9 years of professional writing, from 1-page newsletters to 300-page dissertation
Marketing techniques	Have sold extensive product line for stationery company; also marketed my ideas, talents, and writing during graduate study.

One more hint: Many of the books we've seen have the word "I" beginning almost every paragraph of a cover letter. Obviously, this letter is to introduce yourself, but please remember that the company representative is mostly interested in how you can help the company. A list of "I" sentences may be easy to write, but it's monotonous to read and does not always apply to what the company needs. Be creative; remove the word "I" as much as possible and aim your message at them. Better yet, use the words "we" or "us"—they have a nice inclusive ring that the lonely "I" message misses, such as, "With our needs and talents combined, we would produce a winning team in your marketing division."

The bottom line of résumés and cover letters is that you need to convey a large amount of pertinent information in a small space, you want to stand out from the rest of the competition, whether it's language style or presentation, and you want to be the person who ultimately lands the job. In the following chapters, we continue to encourage you to apply this information in your job search, the interview process, negotiating, and even evaluating the final job offers.

When your résumé is letter-perfect (but not forever—it's usually considered to be a work-in-progress), you can write to all your friends that hanging in there to complete that doctorate was worthwhile after all.

Reference

U. S. Department of Labor. (1998). *Occupational outlook handbook.* Indianapolis, IN: JIST Works, Inc.

PART IV

CHAPTER 10

Perfecting Interview Skills

"I know you believe you understand what you think I asked, but I'm not sure you realize that what you said is not what I asked for."

The interview process should be viewed with excitement, as a wonderful opportunity to show off your finely tuned talents quietly. It's simply an exchange of information for the purpose of exploring your viability as an employee. Some folks, however, get so nervous they end up blinking in bewilderment, like the confused conversationalist in the quotation above. Interviews do not have to be scary if you think of them in the right perspective. As one human resource specialist advised, "An interview is simple communication, a mutual sharing of information. A positive attitude, an air of poise and confidence, shows the minute you walk in my door."

Please ignore any nervous twitches that play into old fears about believing you do not speak well enough to impress anyone, you can't think fast on your feet (or sitting down, either), you won't give the right answers, or your vocal cords will simply freeze with panic from the moment you face an interviewer. None of this will happen if you remember your powerful skills as a communicator, thinker, researcher, and team player. If you wish, gather a group of fellow students or instructors and role-play the interview process; it's guaranteed to produce a few hearty laughs, and that's the best beginning of all.

You will succeed at interviewing by approaching it like your academic career: Do your homework first, and do it thoroughly. Then put on your "Just Do It" mind-set and show the interviewer how great you are. This should be easy for an academician, but many folks, eager to put any activities behind them that resemble tedious graduate assignments, think a civil war is about to erupt.

However, we have found former students who are so tired of the academic demands that they adopt a "what-the-heck" attitude and decide to saunter into an interview with an "I'll just wing it" mentality. This is understandable after the rigors of comprehensive exams and a dissertation "defense" (we're all exhausted veterans of such warlike language), but the casual attitude is neither advisable nor necessary when conducting interviews.

Don't wing it! Being a veteran of the academic process will help you immensely with the preparation phase, so stay positive. You certainly understand the research process, so put these skills to good use. This time you're going to focus your research in three areas: on yourself, identifying your skills, talents, and personality traits; on the companies in which you are interested; and on the actual interview process.

Let's back up for a moment and think through the big picture. What's the purpose of an interview? For the interviewee, it's to sell your skills, knowledge, and personality to the representative of the company so that he or she will recognize what a valuable contribution you will bring to the organization. Then you will be hired for a reasonable salary into a position that suits you and the company and offers you a chance for advancement. Of course, other issues count, too, such as helping the company grow. Remember the hiring manager's mantra: Hire for Personality, Train for Skill.

Three Basic Questions

The interviewer has three basic questions that must be answered:

1. Do your skills fit the position? (Can you do this job? What will you contribute?)

2. Will you be an addition to the company culture? (Do you fit in?)

3. Will you perform your duties for a reasonable salary? (How much do I have to pay this person?) Hint: You already can see that the word *reasonable* can create terror at the financial negotiating table. But more on that later.

The goal of a successful interview, of course, is for everybody to win. The result, unfortunately, can range from wonderful wins to hand-wringing wipe outs.

In this chapter, we cover the first two—Can You Do the Job? and Will You Fit In? The third item, Negotiating Your Salary, is a big and often frightening hurdle for even the most experienced of job seekers, and it is your last moment of independence before signing on the dotted line; we address it in the next chapter.

Who Am I?

The first set of questions belongs to you: Who Are You? Most students have put so much time into absorbing and then spitting out information about every major contributor to their particular field of study that they don't take the time or have the energy to turn the spotlight on their own talents. And, of course, there's a little gender-bender issue here that we need to think about. Although men generally tend to have no trouble spelling out their multiple talents (and even enjoy embellishing on occasion for dramatic or appealing effect, living out a joyful "King of the Hill" mentality), women often have a difficult time tooting their own horns, having more of a "Hide Head in the Sand" mentality nourished from childhood. The interview is exactly when we do have to toot our horns about skills, talents, problem-solving experiences, conflict management techniques, or any other question thrown at us. If we don't speak up for ourselves, who will? So whatever your gender or personality, this is the time to broadcast your skills to the interviewer.

It's difficult to analyze ourselves objectively, and although we may be able to ramble for hours about our research findings or work skills, we are often reluctant to discuss our particular personality traits. Or we may think everyone is like us, so why talk about it? That's the whole point: Everyone is not like us. We are each unique, and although we may share talents with others we know, we still have different ways of presenting ourselves. So talk about yourself—not for hours on end, of course, boring everyone to tears like your crotchety old Uncle Fred used to do at family dinners, but speak just long enough to sell your talents and personality to the hiring manager or human resources person.

Then, when the infamous opening gambit pops out of the interviewer's mouth—"Tell me about yourself"—you will have accurate answers available without hemming and hawing. (We'll show you more about how to do this later in the chapter—this is the teaser.)

The major issue here lies in the confusion most people have in identifying *transferable skills* and separating them from *personality traits*. And yes, there is a big difference between the two. Skills are the abilities you have acquired by living, learning, and working in the world, they are transferable to different settings, and they are the basics of your work. Skills are things you do well, like to do, and seek out for gainful employment or enjoyable leisure activity, such as negotiating, counseling, motivating, measuring, interpreting, and researching.

Personality traits, however, are considered to be inborn (although they surely have been developed along the way) and include attributes such as energy, dedication, enthusiasm, flexibility, creativity, humor, and cooperativeness. The personality trait list is usually much longer than the skill list, but it is equally valuable. Several employers have told us they are more interested in learning the applicant's personality traits; they can teach or improve any necessary skills.

In your personal assessment, you may wish to consider taking one of the personality tests mentioned in Chapter 2 if you haven't already done so. The beauty of the personality analyses is that they offer language and ideas that lead you into positive discussions during an interview. For a shy, quiet grad student, it may be easier to talk about oneself with a lead-in such as, "On the Myers-Briggs, my personality type is an ISTJ." If the interviewer has no clue what you are talking about—and this is not only possible, but probable, depending on where you are interviewing—the next discussion is all yours. You now have a chance to be clever, illuminating, and succinct. And please do be succinct—putting an interviewer to sleep is never recommended.

After you have some of your winning personality traits down pat, start thinking about your particular skills. Focus on transferable skills—the traits you learned in the academic process that can be transferred to a business workplace. This is a key issue, because many people tend to think the world of academics and the world of commerce function on two different wavelengths.

"Ah," gripe the harried business folks, "you folks in the ivory towers just play with theories and esoteric ideas; you have no idea what it's like to be on the front lines having to make fast decisions involving people's lives or millions of dollars."

To which the smooth-talking ivory tower voices retort, "We're dealing with vital concepts that guide your decisions; don't you recognize our value?"

The arguments are silly and unsolvable, so you must be ready to bridge the gap. When migrating from academics to business, you take with you many powerful talents from your student experiences that can be transferred easily into a variety of work environments. Make a detailed list of your skills and be ready for the likely question "What skills do you bring to our workplace?" And you can readily answer, "I have extensive research, abstract reasoning, and analysis skills that are invaluable in a marketing department" or "Problem solving is one of my strongest and most accurate skills, and this fits into any company arena." Another good response is, "I have flexible interpersonal skills that will contribute to successful communications for your human resource department."

Often, you will be asked to give an example, so of course you will have stories:

> I recognized a problem with the information flow from faculty to students. I designed a computerized template acceptable to professors that could easily be accessed by, or given to, students, and then installed the template into the graduate office computers and offered free disks for student use. This saved time and increased the efficiency of student-professor communication.

Just think of yourself leaping tall buildings in a single bound, and you're the hero of the day. Or of any day.

Suppose you are asked, "What is the best strength you have to offer us?" You may be tempted to answer just one, but don't be shy if you're feeling comfortable—link a couple of other closely related strengths into your answer. You may answer with three, such as, "My best strength is problem-solving, and combined with my flexibility and love of seeing a challenge through to the end, I do very well in this area." You are sounding strong and articulate because you thought about this carefully, made lists of your strongest skills, asked others for feedback, and now you are eager to discuss them with the interviewer. Why stop at the mention of only one talent when three or four intertwined talents, spit out in an articulate row, will make an even better impression?

Another "who am I" analysis is to focus on what it is you want to do, and this is where the "data, people, and things" areas (which we discussed in Chapter 1) need to be understood and articulated. You have dealt with all three in graduate school: You analyzed enormous amounts of data, stumbled through a maze of bewildering personalities, and were forced to organize all the physical aspects of your environment. But which arena do you like best or function in best? You're a big kid now; you should be able to recognize these immediately.

One of the questions many career counselors enjoy asking their clients is, "If I could wave a magic wand, and if I offered you the chance to do any three things you wanted without regard to finances, location, or any restrictions, what would you like to do?" We always encourage clients to think creatively, as freely as possible. The answers are often quite revealing, such as the response from the outspoken young man who announced he wanted to "own his own country" (and got a big laugh in response). When we evaluate all three choices of a client, there is usually a common thread running through the answers that identifies one or more key personality traits.

For instance, the fellow who wanted to own his own country actually wanted to create and run his own electronic business and be able to choose where he could live with his wife and young family. The common thread was clear: He wanted to be in control of his own destiny, and he was willing to take the responsibility for his own decisions. That led to a discussion of identifying his traits and recognizing other abilities that fit into the dominant theme. A dependable, solid worker indeed—with prized attributes for a future employer. He's close to being his own boss.

Now that you have a good idea of what buzzwords you need for an interview, let's move on to the interview process itself. We separate this topic into six categories:

1. Preparing for the interview

2. Dressing for, driving to, and drying sweaty palms before the interview

3. Conducting informational interviews

4. The actual (gulp) interview and questions that may and may not be asked

5. Telephone screening interviews (which are becoming more common)

6. Group interviews—definitely not the warm fuzzies

Preparing for the Interview

There are four concepts to understand for this phase: homework, homework, homework, homework. The beginning step is to start a file—a nice, clean, lightweight, unobtrusive manila file that will travel with you to all appointments. No sloppy, unwieldy backpacks, no scruffy canvas totes with papers falling out the sides, no tattered briefcases. One folder. Call it your *Famous Flimsy Folder.* We'll tell you what to put in it; for now, it's smart just to have one handy.

Your first assignment is to find out the exact job description for the position you think you are interested in, including the expectations and salary range. Finding this information depends on how you initially heard about the opening. If you learned about it through a friend or someone in the company, you have a giant head start—that person will be able to help you get a beginning description of job responsibilities and give you the name of the hiring manager. If you read about a position in the newspaper, your search will take a little longer, and your competition will be stiffer, but the same process applies.

Your second assignment is to check your résumé (Chapter 9) and see if a little tweaking will make you sound like a hotter prospect. Obviously, you can't tweak the academic or work history—fudging facts is definitely not allowed, and they can be, and are, often checked—but because you've included unique skills and your wonderful personality traits on your résumé, you might want to put those in a different order so a hiring manager or human resource representative will find the necessary qualifications quickly. Our personal preference is to see a résumé written in such a solid and thorough style that it can go anywhere without tweaking, unless, of course, you are seeking a wide variety of positions in corporate or government settings. Then you may even need separate résumés. Is patience one of your admirable traits?

The third assignment is to make a list of your personal assets that match the ones requested in the job listing. If they are looking for someone with analytical skills, write down an example of how you have and use yours. If the job requires flexible hours, write down how grad school taught you to sleep days, study and write at nights when your abode was quiet, or give up sleep entirely. If this position requests financial experience, surely your creative accounting to pay school bills will fit in here somewhere. The key is to have these stories ready when you sit down with an interviewer.

The fourth and final assignment (sounds like a syllabus, doesn't it?) is to do your research on the company long before you ever walk in the door. An enormous amount of valuable information is on the Internet, in library resource sections, and in local publications. How long have they been in business? Are they big enough to be on a stock exchange, and, if so, what is their financial position? What is their product, their goal, their culture, their hiring history? What is their salary history for this position?

Much of this information can be found on the company Web site. It seems that everyone, from single-owner businesses to multinational corporations, has a Web site packed with company information. Use it, and then when the interviewer asks you, "Do you have any questions about our company?" you will have your question list available in your Famous Flimsy File, which you always will carry with you to an interview. We'll give you lots of sample questions later in this chapter.

The Actual Interview: Dressing, Driving, and Preventing Sweaty Palms

How to dress for an interview is one of the most common questions career counselors get asked. And there is only one standard answer: Dress one step above what the other people are wearing. The problem with this answer is that you don't usually know how the people in any given company dress, so you have to fall back on common sense. So we have another answer: Dress in a professional manner.

The professional gurus who train folks for these forays into the job search process advise that professional dress means, for women, either a business suit (with skirt or pants, just make sure you have a three-piece outfit), a minimum of jewelry, a minimum of make-up, and clean, tidy hairstyle. For men, it means a business suit, a sport coat if the office is casual, and well-groomed hair. If you have pierced body parts with dangling protest messages, and (for males) an extraordinarily long ponytail, you may or may not be considered professional, depending on the position you are applying for and the company culture. We suggest you investigate the company culture thoroughly before you walk in for an interview appointment, and dress accordingly.

Remember the old adage, "You don't get a second chance to make a first impression"? Well, this is your first impression: how you look. Before you open your mouth, your "look" speaks volumes. Make it work for you.

We recently spoke with a young man who was well dressed and had a full head of below-the-ribs-length blond hair in a ponytail. He'd been "downsized" and was job hunting. His biggest complaint wasn't that he had to seek another position—he was confident about his skills—but that he knew he'd have to cut his hair. "My friends know how long I've been with a company by the length of my hair," he laughed. "I cut my hair for the initial interviews, then once I'm hired I never cut it again. I was with the last company 6 years, and this is how long it grew." He was saddened, but prepared, to go to a barber. He knew what professional appearance called for and was willing to make the sacrifice.

Now that you are neat and tidy, you need to get yourself to the interview. Do everyone a favor and make a dry run, unless you know exactly where you're going. See how long it takes you to get to the location, and know which building/entrance/office you are going to. Then, when the actual interview is scheduled, get there early enough to smooth out clothing wrinkles and jangly nerves. Neither you nor the interviewer is going to get off to a good start if your frantic, late arrival louses up his or her schedule.

For nervousness, breathe. Three deep breaths, then three more. Breathing is the one thing people actually forget to do when nervous. As for the classic complaint of sweaty palms, we have absolutely no advice on how to eliminate sweaty palms if this is part of your persona. But we do know many people worry about how temporarily stressful times create hot, damp palms, and this is understandable. The instinct is to quickly rub them on your pants and skirt, and we really don't see anything wrong with this. You certainly can't wipe them on the furniture, or on the receptionist. (But you could try talcum powder or antiperspirant on those sweaty palms.)

Some people claim they hold a tissue to sop up the nervousness, but you can't shake hands that way, and if you try to stuff a damp tissue in your pocket but instead drop it on the floor, then where are you? Bending over and looking pretty silly when you're supposed to be standing tall, shaking hands, and maintaining direct eye contact. The ideal situation, of course, is to be so prepared, both in your head and in the flimsy file you are carrying, that the sweaty palms will disappear with the three deep breaths you are taking and you won't have to worry about them anymore.

A few other suggestions are in order. Go alone to the interview. Arrive early. And be extremely courteous to everyone you meet. A young receptionist recently told us a story about how she had been treated in a brusque and demeaning manner from a fellow dropping off his résumé prior to his interview the next day. When the human resource manager asked her opinion of this man, she was honest about his rudeness. "I am part of this company too," she complained. The HR person made a mental note of this, and the next day, when he repeated the rudeness, she told him that their company members treated every level of employee equally and she didn't think he would fit into the company culture.

Remember the second question of the interviewer, to see if you would fit into the company culture? The applicant above learned a painful but obviously necessary lesson when he didn't even get an interview for that position.

A caveat here: Not all interviewers are created equally, nor should they be. In an extended search, you will most likely run into some terrific, easy-to-talk-to, cozy, warm-and-fuzzy interviewers, you may run into some ho-hummers who give you no inkling of where you stand, or you may encounter someone so lacking in communication skills that you end up leading the discussion. The ones who will cause all sorts of sweaty body parts, however, are the Take No Prisoners type, using beady stares, bored body language, and sharp, interruptive language to control and intimidate the interviewee. There is no way you will change their style, just do your best to stay calm and unflappable. Breathe deeply, present your skills and positive traits, and then move on to the next interview.

Conducting Informational Interviews

An informational interview has one primary purpose: to gain knowledge about a company or business you would like to investigate as a potential employer. As a recent or about-to-be graduate, you probably have many questions about the world outside academics, and this is an excellent way to get information.

The answers you are seeking include learning more about a field you are interested in pursuing, figuring out if your talents and interests match that company, and making contacts within the company that may be useful later. Some people have told us that their information interviews also yielded nuggets of information about some not-yet-advertised or upcoming vacancies within the company, and they felt they were on an inside track to put in an application. A few found the most ideal of all situations: They asked for an informational interview, found the interaction to be exciting and rewarding, and then discovered that the "information only" interview was quietly and casually turning into a job interview. Two of our friends were hired on the spot. A rare but plausible occurrence.

Now the big question is, how do you sign up for an informational interview? It's not like a graduate class, in which you call in with your student number or stand in lines and pay huge fees, thank heavens, but it does involve that tiresome process of homework. First, run to your nearest college or university career center and start questioning everyone in sight. Read the resources they suggest, and there are many comprehensive directories available. See if alumni are coming in for talks, or if there is a list of alumni who are willing to share information on a phone call. Get on the Internet and look into sites like careermosaic.com, monsterboard, and the many others available (see Appendix C for extensive Internet listings).

What you are looking for is the name of someone within the company who will give you 15 or 20 minutes of precious time to tell you what their work world is like. Once you have a name, either write them ahead of time or simply call them to request a meeting time. And, of course, you will say you are only seeking information. Ask them for advice and counsel, powerful words that most people can't refuse.

Will You Fit In?

The information interview is an excellent situation to assess your "fit" into the company culture. It gives you a chance, in a relaxed environment, to get a good feel for the people, the work expectations, and the skills needed—all your sticky questions.

Here are some areas you may wish to explore—and you have a list already prepared and handy and ready to pull from your Famous Flimsy File:

INFORMATIONAL INTERVIEW SAMPLE QUESTIONS

1. Would you describe your typical work day?
2. When did you first become interested in this line of work?
3. What unique abilities or skills do you feel help you in this work?
4. What are your work responsibilities?
5. What 3 or 4 tasks consume 80% of your time?
6. To whom do you answer—a supervisor, a manager? How do they communicate?
7. What are the hours? Any flexibility allowed?
8. What are the opportunities for growth/promotion? What is the turnover?
9. How do people treat one another? Technology-oriented or relationship-based?
10. If you could change something about your job, what would it be?
11. Do you have any recommendations for a new kid on the block like me?

Now exit. Stick to the time frame you agreed to, and then thank the person by name for sharing his or her time and valuable information. You may ask if he or she might have any other recommendations or resources for you to investigate, then skedaddle out of there and collapse in your car in a happy heap. (I was once so excited after leaving one of these interviews that I set off my car alarm in the parking lot and suddenly couldn't remember the code to turn it off. At least it happened AFTER the interview. And eventually I did get a terrific unadvertised position. Don't you love happy endings?)

Because you have such excellent note-taking skills, whip out that pen and pad of paper, and, while sitting in your car, write down the name and title of the person with whom you spoke, the company name, and all information you garnered. If you sensed a particular niche or area in which your skills would fit, write this down—and bring it up when you get a real interview, or save it for future reference.

What's your final exam in an informational interview? Write a thank-you note. Sounds corny, but the old-fashioned rules still apply. The human resources professionals advise, "Don't write me a letter on e-mail, don't leave a quick message on my machine. Write me a short, pleasant thank you note—three sentences, if that's all you can muster—and put it on small, non-gaudy stationery. I've hired people based on this courtesy." If the folks who hire like this professional touch, why ignore it?

There are two questions that clients tell us, and that we have read, are always asked at an interview. The first is, "Tell me about yourself."

"I *hate* that question!" groan many experienced interviewees. "I never know what to say, and it makes me so nervous. What do they want to hear?"

What they want to hear is what you have to sell: your major skills and personality traits that match what they are seeking. Remember that summary statement you created in your nifty new résumé in Chapter 9? The one with three sentences that summed up your entire adult professional life? The résumé books agree that your summary statement is the perfect answer for this question because it answers three areas: length of time in the workforce, strong skills, and valuable personality traits. The interviewer can take it from there—you've just given him or her a variety of concise information to expand on at will.

The second ever-popular stumper question is, "Why should we hire you?" or, phrased more politely, "What best qualifies you for this position?" Because you have already done extensive homework on both the company and the advertised position, you know what they are looking for, so you answer accordingly. If they want someone who programs computers, and their dress code is usually shorts, T-shirt, and flip-flops (don't you wonder what they wear on "casual" days?), and you're a computer wizard, then tout your computer expertise (no need to mention your dislike of dressing up). If they want someone for marketing who can test baseball bats in the back property, then bring out all your experience in baseball leagues and sales. If they are looking for someone who can step into a training situation with little or no preparation, then tell about your wildly successful extemporaneous speeches in classes and how much you love the freedom and creativity of improvisation.

In other words, whatever they want is what you will honestly tell about. The key is: Answer the question! Give as well-rounded, concise, and representative a response as you can. And, because you are so well prepared from the questions you'll get in this and other books, you'll be able to tell them exactly why you should be hired.

How long should you talk when answering a question? Two minutes, max. The trademark of a seasoned interviewee is making responses short, sweet, and accurate. Use the person's name often—we all love to hear our own names—and try to keep from fidgeting or giggling or scratching or staring at the floor.

As for the questions you might get asked, we have hundreds. In the interest of your sanity and ours, we'll try to shorten that to a few general sample questions in each area. If you want to expand these, pick up some of the excellent books on the market or in your library that deal with this topic. A few favorites of ours are *Knock 'Em Dead—With Great Answers to Tough Interview Questions,* by Martin John Yate, and *Sweaty Palms: The Neglected Art of Being Interviewed,* by Anthony Medley, but there are many more in your local bookstores.

More Sample Questions

The questions most often asked by employers fall into four general categories:

◆ Work Experience

◆ Your Potential Role in Their Company

◆ Your Education

◆ And a category we happily refer to as Miscellaneous, which means anything can pop out (the section on questions you ask of a potential employer appeared previously in this chapter).

WORK EXPERIENCE

1. How does your previous work experience relate to this job?
2. What have you done that shows initiative and willingness to work?
3. What did you most enjoy about your previous work? What did you least enjoy?
4. What suggestions have been given to you to improve your performance?
5. Have you ever worked as part of a team?
6. How do you handle a situation in which one member of the team is not working to your level of expectation?
7. What two or three accomplishments gave you the greatest satisfaction?
8. What's the worst mistake you made on the job, and how did you handle it?
9. What have you learned from your mistakes?
10. What would your last employer say about your work style?
11. How do you organize and plan for major projects?
12. How do you handle conflicting priorities?

YOUR POTENTIAL ROLE IN THIS COMPANY

1. Why do you want to work for our company?
2. What do you know about our financial/cultural/environmental side?
3. What three things are most important to you in your work?
4. What is your idea of how our industry works?
5. How does this position fit into your career path?
6. What contributions can you make to this department?
7. Why should I hire you for this position?
8. Can you supervise people? How do you know?
9. What do you think you will most like about this job? What do you think you will least like?
10. Which is more important to you—the money or the type of work?

EDUCATION

1. Why did you choose this career?
2. How has your graduate education prepared you for this position?
3. Why did you choose your particular doctoral program?
4. What was your most difficult subject? What was the easiest?
5. What percentage of your education expenses did you earn? (Or, how much debt have you incurred?)
6. What would a former professor tell me about you?
7. Do you feel your GPA is related to your future work style?
8. Do your career goals include postdoctoral study?
9. How would you relate your academic successes to your career goals?
10. Do you think in ivory tower terms, or can you adjust to the "real world"?

MISCELLANEOUS

1. Tell me about yourself.
2. What are your 6-month, 5-year, or 10-year goals?
3. Give me an example of a major problem you have solved.
4. Give an example of how you responded to a professional criticism.
5. How would you resolve conflict in a group situation?
6. How do you evaluate success?
7. What do you think it takes to be successful in this company?
8. How do you work when under deadlines or pressure?
9. Why do you want to work for this company?
10. Describe the relationship that should exist between a supervisor and those who report to her or him.

There are some other questions that are considered illegal to ask in an interview, but that doesn't stop companies from putting those same questions on an application form. We have no idea of the legal ramifications of this tactic, and we don't want to slide down that slippery slope, but we do want you to be aware that there are some questions that should never be asked in an interview. Some of these nonquestions concern the following:

◆ Age

◆ Race or ethnic background

◆ Drug or alcohol use

◆ Marital or parental status

◆ Arrest record

◆ Child care plans

If these questions are asked, and you are uncomfortable with them (some people are not), your best recourse is to ask how this question pertains to your application or ability to do the job. Also, try to answer everything positively. A single mother we know with two grade-school children always mentions this topic herself, and then tells the interviewer, "I have excellent child care, and a backup system in place, so I have never missed a day of graduate school or work because of child care problems." She feels this gets the issues out in the open and deflected before concerns can be raised. "It's always worked for me," she added. "It's a question that begs an answer, so I give it first."

We recommend you do whatever is comfortable for you, but an awareness of these potentially illegal questions can't hurt. Jan once was in an interview in which the hiring person announced that he was concerned about her age and her willingness to do the work because she had other professional, but part-time, commitments. She could have sued his insensitive little neck, but instead she challenged him to give her a chance to prove him wrong. It worked out, and they both laugh about it now, but it was quite uncomfortable at the time.

If you get asked any questions about former coworkers, supervisors, professors, or anyone with whom you have worked or schooled, we suggest you do not use this opportunity to spill your guts about all your frustrations. Now is the time to act cool and, if necessary, simply say, "We didn't always see eye-to-eye on issues, but we always worked things out amicably." Chances are as soon as you bad-mouth someone, the interviewer will smile and admit, "That's my brother-in-law." Negative answers will always come back to haunt you, so why bother?

A final question that may be tossed at you without warning is, "What's your biggest weakness?" Be prepared for this, think about it ahead of time, and have a positive response ready. Mention whatever you think may have been a weakness, but then tell how you learned from it and made it a positive experience. A frequent one we hear is, "My coworkers tell me I'm a workaholic, but I like to do what is necessary to see a project through to completion." Or, in the people business, "I worry a lot about the employees in my department, but we have excellent communication skills and now can resolve most problems." Your motto is to accentuate the positive and eliminate the negative at every opportunity.

And while you are carefully being evaluated by the hiring personnel, what is your responsibility? To interview them right back. That's why the interview is a mutual exchange of information. You need to see how well you would fit into this environment. You may never have had that choice before. Once you signed into a graduate program, hopefully for the right reasons, you were in it until you quit or graduated. Worrying about a "fit" wasn't a concern, you just followed the "yellow book road."

But in looking for a position of employment in the business world, the fit is far more important. What is important to you for job satisfaction at a professional level? Begin with examining the industry as a whole. Does it mesh with your financial or environmental or personal value system? Are you a Greenpeace member applying for a position in a company that is being sued for dumping chemicals into local riverbeds? What are the growth prospects of this industry, and how dependent are they on current business or governmental policies? If you are going into computer technology areas, the future mind-set is especially important. At least a few educated guesses would help guide you. If you're interested in sales or marketing, what does your research tell you about the future of the company product(s)?

The next step is to explore the individual company or companies to see if you fit in the corporate culture. Do they espouse nonprofit status or pay silly little salaries when you are wanting a fast-track to sleek limousines and private yachts? Do you need intellectual stimulation, challenge, the opportunity to use your academic credentials, a chance for rapid or scheduled advancement, or time to be alone to work at your own pace? Does this position match the most cherished aspects of your personality?

When you narrow the list to a few targeted companies, your research becomes more detailed. You'll want to learn as much as possible about the inner workings of both the company product and the people. If they are technically creative, offering a high-quality product or service, with excellent management style and financial stability, and if they seem to be filling a customer need, you're heading in the right direction. Now all you need to find out are the stated goals for growth, the established reputation in the market-place, the personnel policies, and salary and benefits.

Time for a bedtime story. A young man with distinguished academic cre-dentials interviewed with the marketing department of a large research com-pany. The first two interviews went perfectly. Clearly, he could do the job, and he seemed to fit in perfectly. The third meeting was scheduled for salary negotiation and to meet other members of the department. These functions also went smoothly, and the supervisor invited the group to lunch in a nearby restaurant.

The supervisor then yelled at the young waitress, insulted her serving abilities, and embarrassed her throughout the meal. "It was so sad," the young man told us. "He laughed about his treatment of her, and the others, who would be my future coworkers, also laughed. They kept saying, 'Oh that Joe, he's such a tease, what will he do next?'"

The young man didn't wait to find out what "Joe" would do next. He returned to Joe's office and then quietly told him he could not work in an en-vironment of hostility in which people made fun of others. "We simply don't fit," he said. His discomfort with the company culture was so strong he walked away from an attractive salary.

It's not difficult to discover if you will fit into a company culture. All you need to do is look around you, listen to others, and use your intuition. One friend of ours, a former executive with a large insurance company and now a life change consultant, recommends eating lunch in the company cafeteria or standing around at break time or in the parking lot, casually asking folks about the firm. You will quickly get a feeling for the personality of a com-pany. There are very few, if any, jobs that are worth abandoning your value system and adding ulcers to your profile.

Telephone Interviews

Telephone interviews are primarily screening processes, and they are becom-ing more popular due to the enormous numbers of people seeking employ-ment and the overburdened responsibilities of human resource departments. They usually occur after you have sent a résumé to a company and are plan-ning to keep in touch to monitor the progress of your application.

How do you handle them? As professionally as you do every other inter-view. Because you will probably be receiving this call at home, make sure you're in a quiet spot so you can talk freely. And have that Famous Flimsy File near the phone—now is not the time to be sputtering "Wait a minute" and madly searching for your list of questions—in case you get the opportunity to even ask them. This is one advantage of being on the phone—you can read right off your résumé or questions list.

It is appropriate to ask if more than one person is on the line, and, if so, ask them to give their names and identify their role or position. Then you can use each name when you hear that voice on the speakerphone.

Public speaking teachers will all tell you the same thing: When talking on the telephone, stand up. Does Bruce Springsteen or Barbra Streisand or Randy Travis or the Spice Girls sing sitting down? Nope—and you shouldn't talk sitting down if you want your voice to be at its best. Stand up, which will help your breathing, which will help your confidence, which will lead to improved speaking skills. Easy, eh? You already know all the questions to be prepared for, and have your lists handy, so this should be a success story.

Except that it is difficult to carry on such an important conversation when you can't see the other person. No friendly handshakes to calm nerves, no body language signals to interpret, no smiles to increase confidence. But you may not have a choice, so stand tall and speak slowly and comfortably. Then ask for a face-to-face interview.

Group Interviews

There are several names for a group interview, few of which are friendly or positive. These frequently are a ritualized, programmed, cold interview process that is focused entirely on your skills and accomplishments. They are designed to eliminate any biases that may occur in an individual interview setting, so anywhere from 3 to 12 people sit behind a long table facing you in the lonely seat in front of them. They have scripted questions, and they will take turns asking them of you.

One young woman laughed about her recent group interview. "I answered the first question they asked, then quickly mentioned the name of my school and my degree. The next person in line whined that I'd already answered his question, and I wasn't supposed to do that!"

These interviews are used in all areas, but they are especially popular in local and national government programs. Schools districts are using them more often, as are some larger companies. These are not usually the warm-fuzzy interviews you may wish, but you have no choice. You do, however, have a right to ask, when your interview is scheduled, if it will be a group interview and how many people will be present. At least that gives your nerves a chance to revolt and then calm down before you even reach the building.

The same suggestions apply when in a group interview, which some claim feels more like an interrogation than an interview. Jot down the interviewers' names as they introduce themselves so you can address them by proper name (and you'll know to whom to send thank-you cards). When one person asks a question, establish a "personal" contact with the questioner, then do an eye-sweep of the panel as you answer the question, ending back with the original individual. If uncomfortable with this, practice in a role-play with folks at home or roommates. After all the presentations you have given in graduate school, you probably do this without thinking. But be sure to look professional and comfortable in that group interview.

And what about that ubiquitous flimsy file we keep mentioning and advising you to carry with you at all times? This is what we recommend you put in it:

YOUR FAMOUS FLIMSY FILE

◆ Two or more copies of your résumé

◆ A list of questions you wish to ask (based on your research)

◆ Copies of credentials, certificates, and letters of recommendation

◆ Plain paper for note taking (a small pad will do)

◆ Any work samples for which you may be asked (graphic artists carry big files)

We leave this chapter with an overview of the interview process, a checklist to get you through it.

Interview Checklist

1. Review skills and traits.

2. Research companies where you'd like to work.

3. Prepare for interview:

   Complete research.
   Review your own questions.
   Rehearse strength stories.

4. Schedule informational interviews.

5. Dress professionally.

6. Bring Flimsy File.

7. Arrive early.

8. Relax.

CHAPTER 11

Sharpening Negotiation Skills

"Give me the strength to negotiate the things I can, the patience to accept the things I cannot negotiate, and the chance to learn, grow, and earn good money to make it all worthwhile."

Negotiating is an art form that takes practice and preplanning, although some do come by the process naturally. We haven't met many people over the years, however, who brag about their negotiation skills, unless they are in the used car sales business or are one of those tough-minded, "my way or the highway" people of the business, legal, or other high-stake professions.

Negotiation does not assume a prominent process in most graduate programs, and many newly minted doctors in humanities or soft sciences (or most any other field, for that matter) have little or no experience negotiating their professional needs. Once we have been accepted in a graduate program, we're like drones marching to an academic drumbeat: Read the program requirements, buy these books, follow this syllabus, accept that professor, complete the required assignments, follow the protocol, complete the checklist, and graduate.

About the only negotiation possible is for an extended time limit or perhaps a feeble attempt to improve a questionable grade, but even then the process is at the discretion of someone else in the power position. (If we remained on a tenure track in academia, of course, we'd learn negotiation skills in a hurry, for no career is without its share of political maneuvering.

But like students in most school programs, we experience very little opportunity, except, perhaps, in a business program in which negotiation is taught as an elevated art form.)

In official terms, *negotiation* often is defined as a communication process with the goal of reaching agreement on the exchange of goods, services, salaries, reviews, team projects, or whatever is in question. Negotiation begins with a question or conflict, and it ends—ideally—in mutual agreement. Some people think negotiation takes place only while people are sitting primly at long, dark polished tables, with strict rules, scowling bosses, and no breaks. Not true—we actually negotiate with ourselves and others all the time, although we may not realize it. "I think I'll write that paper tonight," you say. "No, this is the night I promised my body I'd haul it to the gym, and no muscles are protesting, so I'll do that and then get up at 5 tomorrow morning to write that paper." We may not think of these exchanges as negotiations, but they are.

In fact, outside of graduate school requirements, we negotiate constantly. We "bargain" with ourselves or others—what to have for meals, where to live, how to balance the budget, what we share, do, buy, lease, and sell. We negotiate so often that we don't even realize we're doing it. We're experienced in this give-and-take process, but when it comes to a formal negotiation for something serious—like our entire future—we suddenly get the shakes and mumbles.

Each of us has our own style of dealing with conflict, which can vary depending on the situation. Deciding whether to have a chocolate sundae is a bit less conflicting than negotiating for a new car. Some revel in the challenges, actively seeking to negotiate anything under the sun. In fact, some of these folks have been known to create conflict just to get issues on the table or because they love to see fur fly. Others simply shrug their shoulders and deal with issues as they pop up; a few literally panic at the mere mention or hint of a conflict and either run away or are suddenly struck mute.

Conflict takes many forms, ranging from ritualized and idolized, as in many sports; to noisy and deadly, as in wars; or to utterly silent, for those who refuse to engage or communicate. Conflict can be casual, fun, creative, productive, frustrating, painful, or life-threatening. The only way out of conflicted situations, however, is by decree or by negotiation. Negotiation is better.

Negotiations usually will be successful if all parties believe in honesty and try to understand the other person's position, but how often does this happen? Let's be honest about this: Most of the time, the involved parties are trying to make the best deal they can for themselves. There's no shortage of the "What's in it for me?" mentality in our world today. If you are a practicing mediator/negotiator, however—a role becoming more popular in a wide range of professions—you will be—or are presumed to be—looking for the most equitable solution for both parties. (The obvious exception to this are the fellows, and yes, they all seem to be "fellows," who represent sports figures and try to negotiate unheard-of sums of money for dubious or short-lived talents. Mutual benefit is the goal, but everyone else usually pays the exorbitant fees.)

What is your negotiation style? Be in charge, won't give an inch? Proud of yourself if you win and someone else loses? Or maybe you're interested in the win-win philosophy that's bandied about these days or have noble goals that are extremely difficult to reach? We know the "everyone loses" philosophy is never a goal, but, sadly, this often happens in a protracted or selfish process.

Personal Negotiation Styles

The first phase in assessing your style is to think about your attitudes and basic personality style regarding conflict and negotiation. We learned about such topics as infants, and our families had a huge impact on our basic operating style. We're also influenced by our gender, cultural attitudes, and even our birth order. Firstborns are traditionally thought to have a take-charge mentality; middles are often skilled mediators and peacekeepers; lastborns (we call them "cabooses") are often the free-spirited, lighthearted family members. These are broad generalizations, of course, but they have been found so often in family studies that the theories have become fairly well entrenched in current psychological thinking.

If these attitudes are accurate for your own family style, then we would understand if a firstborn was a tough-minded, serious negotiator, willing to take on the difficult challenges and be determined to come out on top. The middles, often referred to as "mediators," might go for the win-win situations and work hard to keep fists from flying, whereas cabooses would tend to maintain a carefree atmosphere as they attempt to keep communications flowing smoothly. We find these theories fit most people we've met and spoken with, and all agree it helps to know your basic personality style before going into a serious negotiation for important decisions such as career, salary, and benefits.

What was your family pattern? What were the family styles of punishment, rewards, attention, and problem solving—open discussions, hide under the bed until the storm blows over, or outright tyranny? We've heard many women say that their families did not consult them about issues in conflict, and they were never allowed to make decisions for themselves. When the time came to make a career or business negotiation, involving either themselves or their company, many women literally had no experience.

"If I wasn't allowed to decide what school to attend, what to wear, or even how to cut my own hair, how can I survive trying to negotiate a salary or vacation time?" asked one young woman with a fearful expression. "I'd probably just say 'Well, whatever,' and take what they offered with no questions." Another woman said, "I was so tired of job hunting, and so happy to get an offer, I didn't want to jeopardize anything by asking for a negotiation of any kind." Coming to a negotiating table with sharpened skills, an open mind, and positive energy is difficult for those with a history of being controlled, ignored, or put down or for those who are just plain hungry.

Gender is an issue we simply cannot overlook. Research is full of studies discussing the role of women in many current societies, roles whereby women are often socialized to be peacekeepers and to give in for the sake of a smooth resolution to any conflict. The current increase in competitive sports and stand-up-for-yourself language is felt to be helping many women overcome this "ignore it until it goes away" or "I'd rather do it myself than fight about it" mentality, but we have found far more women than men who say, "I'm just no good at this stuff."

In addition, many negotiating books ignore this gender consideration, preferring to lump everyone together in the same rigid boat, with the resulting female comments: "Oh, that book is so male-oriented, I simply cannot adopt those strategies." Other books geared for women's negotiation styles—few and far between, if bookstores are any indication—would probably get an even stronger reaction from men: "No way would I do that!"

Women and men are perceived to have quite different communication styles, and this has been borne out by the avalanche of books in the 1990s discussing gender differences. What we keep reading is the theory that men are felt to take a more forceful, controlled, and even dominating position, based on their general inner-directed personality style. Women are perceived to search for more mutual, connection-oriented solutions, developed from their culturally encouraged outer-directed lifestyles. The results of these differences are particularly noticeable in the negotiation process.

Implications from these gender perceptions may cause a traditional male job-seeker to think, if he's meeting with a woman, "Easy, I can push my position to my advantage." Yet be wary of such assumptions; we've met female supervisors and human resource directors who are the most direct and powerful negotiators we have ever seen; conversely, we've met men who are extremely skillful at using connective ideas and eagerly support a job seeker's goals, an arena thought to be traditionally female. What we are saying is, Negotiator Beware! This is an area in which old assumptions must be put aside, because traditional gender communication styles are a-changing.

A few basic tenets do apply, however. It is well known that women tend to be excellent readers of body language, and this is a powerful tool in any negotiation strategy. Many books advise a job-seeker to mimic the body language of the other person during negotiations; some call it "synchronization," and women find this easy and may do it almost unconsciously (most men I've mentioned this to say, "No way!"). But body language is a powerful tool, sending strong, silent signals that are far more difficult to control than verbal language.

One common communication theory claims that 65% of most communication is body language, 30% is the way people talk, and 5% is the content. Pretty scary, isn't it? You are anticipating having successful work negotiations resulting in a position, a boost in salary, yearly bonuses, stock options, or an extra week of paid vacation, and yet the words aren't coming—or your body language is contradicting the points you are trying to make.

Assess your own style. Are you slumped, round-shouldered, with wavering eye contact and glum facial expressions? Are your head and hands in constant motion? Is your potential boss sitting primly, hands firmly pressed together, staring over your shoulder, or fiddling with papers on the desk? Both your body and his or her position speak volumes and will give you big clues on what to ask for clarification or even how far to push. Big hint here: If you do manage to get the hiring manager or current supervisor to agree to a raise (or whatever the issue), be sure to get it in writing before you leave the office. It's a famous old negotiating trick to promise something that is promptly forgotten a few moments later (think "politician").

Women also tend to trust their intuition about what a person is going to say, how a situation should be handled, and what body language is indicating far more than do men. Women often read body language without thinking about it and are excellent interpreters of head and body messages. Men have the same capabilities, but usually they don't trust the message from their internal computer. I recently heard a president of a large career transition company discuss the need for men, in particular, to learn to "think below the neck" and practice trusting their intuition. If CEOs are beginning to talk this way and are actually willing to "walk the talk," perhaps another gender barrier is breaking down and negotiation meetings and participants will benefit.

"But watch out for the male power pose," one woman laughingly said, as she mimicked that classic male power gesture—elbows on the table, fingers touching and aimed upward. "The 'I'm in charge here and don't you forget it' position—knocks negotiations 10 paces backward." Confident men also have been known to tout their position of power by leaning back in the chair, polished shoes perched on a large desk, with hands crossed casually behind a well-groomed head. "Don't think I'll mimic that pose!" the woman laughed (although we can't help but think it would be worth it for a woman to apply a little "synchronization" and copy the body language, just to see the male reaction. Not in a short skirt, however—or any skirt). One negotiating strategist shared with us his impressions of gender differences at a salary negotiating table. He felt women had a better vision of the big picture, what the salary (or position or title) would mean to the future for both their families and the company, whereas men usually focus on a quick and individual solution. He feels women also see a negotiation as simply a part of the overall working relationship, wanting everyone to win something important to them, whereas men tend to seek individual power and use negotiation to try to convince the other person of his importance. What a difference in styles this creates.

All these issues—family history, birth order, previous experience, goals, gender, cultural training, and even age and positions of power—enter into every negotiating situation. From home to community to workplace, your negotiating style is unique and fairly firmly entrenched. Recognizing your own talents and quirks will work to your advantage; understanding areas in which you are uncomfortable indicates ideas for you to research and practice.

Personality Styles

Many professional negotiators recommend that the person seeking a professional goal try to figure out the quirks and personality style of the negotiator sitting across from him or her. This is easier when involved in protracted discussions, but it also can be helpful when in a quick "Here's the job description, this is the salary, take it or leave it" situation, which is quite common in entry levels of the business world.

There are many books offering assessments and analyses of the different personality types, one of the most popular being the Myers-Briggs Type Indicator with the classic 16 personality styles used so often in business, education, psychology, counseling, and many other arenas (Chapter 2 contains a more detailed description). The standard Myers-Briggs needs to be administered and interpreted by professional consultants, but there is a shorter version called the Keirsey Temperament Test (see keirsey.com) that yields the same 16-personality type analysis, which can be found on the Internet on many sites, including most university Web pages, such as evergreen.edu.

A condensed version of personality assessment, shortened from the original 16-type inventory, has been in use for many years and describes four basic personality styles. Although the four types have been named and renamed depending on the profession using them, many communication and negotiation professionals consider it to be an extremely useful and quick analysis for understanding others.

The most commonly used descriptions of the four basic personality styles are *Aggressive, Analytical, Expressive,* and *Amiable.* These terms are applied in a wide range of endeavors that involve people (as opposed to data and technology), including businesses involving sales, such as real estate, insurance, automobiles, and manufacturing; psychology at all levels and ages; communication courses; teaching programs; and even marital counseling. Most negotiation discussions and/or books will bring up a version of this

---

AGGRESSIVE

The serious, bottom-lined individual, determined to emerge the winner with tough reputation intact and little to no knowledge of the needs or interests of those on the other side of his power position. Talks fast, may raise voice to drown you out—a hierarchical, military style (we say "his" because most men are socialized to be aggressive; some take it to the take-no-prisoners mentality, whereas others are merely bossy. Occasionally, a woman fits this description, which seems to surprise and upset more men than women). Aggressives search for quick answers, few details, your expertise, and are always solution-oriented. They want answers to WHAT you offer them.

ANALYTICAL

The mental gymnast nimbly juggling numbers, facts, figures, sizes, and potential outcomes. Will usually procrastinate until reams of information cover the table. Tends to prefer and trust technology over dealing with real people, will hide behind phones and faxes, thus making face-to-face negotiating difficult. Loves details, written descriptions, and long reports, which helps him or her avoid surprises. Tends to be conservative, obsessive-compulsive. Prefers to think through a situation before making a decision. Often does not trust ideas, intentions, or abilities of others, which is why he or she prefers to rely on data. Looking for answers to HOW questions.

EXPRESSIVE

Energetic, social, intuitive, warm, people-friendly, makes quick decisions. Often presents a dramatic, often exuberant personality with descriptive words and body language. Easy to negotiate with if process is short (to fit short attention spans), fun, and productive. Depending on the company and the position, expressive is a wonderful negotiator if speed and socializing are primary considerations. Likes to make decisions without benefit of paperwork or intricate details, which terrorizes analytical personality. Expressives are looking for WHO will be easiest to work with, who will look at them, how much fun they can have in the process— remember, they are the people-oriented folks.

analysis, and if you're interested you can find out more than the following quick sketch.

In negotiating situations, these common styles are reflected as Aggressive, Analytical, Expressive, or Amiable.

How would you negotiate with each type? It depends on your own personality, of course, and how flexible you are willing to be, but a quick fix is possible.

AMIABLE

Easygoing, pleasant, upbeat, peacekeeper, tends to want everyone and the process to be happy. Enjoys conversations, smiles easily, seeks approval from others. Follows rules, tends not to be impulsive or a risk taker. Negotiations flow smoothly until time for a decision, a difficult process for these gentle folks. (Two hints: Many women are reared to present an amiable appearance, but, with little encouragement, many of them can flip a personality switch and become an expressive or aggressive—the current polite term is "assertive"—personality. Second, know that negotiators from differing cultures may masquerade as Amiables but in fact are savvy Aggressives.) True Amiables are self-appointed caregivers, want everyone happy, and tend to look for WHY answers—rational reasons why a certain solution is important.

To negotiate with an Aggressive: Know your bottom line on all negotiable issues, and be ready to speak up firmly, because you won't be given time to hem and haw. Aggressives love this game, they don't take it personally (neither should you), and they will try to get all the marbles while shooting you down. Stay in your intellectual mode (no emotional stuff here!); stay cool and collected and stand up for yourself.

To negotiate with an Analyst: It's like dealing with a day planner: strictly facts, numbers, logic, and what is on paper (one engineer I know loves his day planner so much that he carries it everywhere, even to a beach picnic on Sunday, and gives it a birthday party every year after he unhappily removes outdated material). Your job is to impress on this obsessive adult how you can help the company and how many talents you bring on board, giving all the precise details about your skills and abilities.

To negotiate with Expressives, also known as Energizer Bunnies: Open with a compliment or question about them to establish a friendly relationship—get personal before professional. Use their names and your sense of humor, and then be ready to pull them gently back to the subject when they zip off onto another topic. They like to move fast, make decisions quickly, and move on to more fun stuff. They are looking for a positive relationship, so show your most personable sides.

To negotiate with an Amiable: Hang loose, you are dealing with the classic middle child, natural pleasers, mediators, peacekeepers. Let them know you too are comfortable playing by the rules and like an atmosphere in which everyone is happy. You may not find many Amiables in tough negotiations, because they don't often strive to be a leader or a decision maker. They are easy to work with, however, so keep smiling when you find yourself in their company.

Because you now have, or are about to have, a doctoral degree, you know nothing is ever as simple as it looks—and neither are people. Putting people into one of four boxes barely scratches the surface of their personalities. However, this brief guide is meant to be used as the real estate mogul told me: "It's a quick and easy way to get a beginning handle on the personalities sitting across the desk, and gives me clues of how to approach and deal with them."

Being familiar with these personality types and knowing that these concepts are used in the "real world" is simply doing your homework and getting ready to approach whatever personality presents itself in a negotiating situation. This information ties in with Chapter 10 on interviewing, of course, because chances are about 99.9% that your career/job interviewer will be the same one with whom you conduct the oh-so-serious hiring and salary negotiations, and it would be helpful to have a handle on his or her personality style.

But this temperament discussion is not limited to the interview and hiring process, because before you fully settle into your challenging new business position, you will be up for a performance review (yes, it's like getting graded all over again—and you thought you were beyond that stuff?) and the possibility of a raise, not to mention all the other negotiable items that go on in any work environment, from money to lunch breaks to time off to team leadership roles to gaining more decision-making powers. Talk about the importance of knowing how and when to negotiate!

Similar Personality Styles, Different Language

There is another common assessment format used in business and industry, usually factored in for negotiations, problem solving, and conflict management. It is also useful for individuals to understand their own basic negotiating style, and although part of it is your individual personality, understanding the differences will help you fine-tune your own negotiating patterns depending on which method best fits the situation.

Think of having a big, gooey, delicious, triple-layered chocolate cake sitting in the middle of the table, with one knife to cut it and a limited number of plates. Now let's see how the different approaches will divide up this cake.

A COMPARISON OF THE TWO NEGOTIATION LANGUAGES

AGGRESSIVE is similar to COMPETITIVE
ANALYTICAL is similar to COLLABORATING
EXPRESSIVE is similar to COMPROMISING
AMIABLE is similar to ACCOMMODATING

COMPETITIVE

Competition is the word most often associated with the negotiating process, and there are many who love a challenge of any size or result. The Competitive cake cutter will try to toss away the knife and saunter out the door with the entire cake in his or her possession. This type of competitive personality tends to show itself early and is, in fact, pounded into little boys from the time they can walk and talk. Most little girls hone their competitive skills in grade school, in both the classroom and the playing fields, only to abandon such traits when their bodies sprout bumps and curves and they are told by the culture (or choose themselves) to get off the athletic fields and go home to paint their fingernails. Fortunately, the joys and challenges of the competitive world are being embraced by many girls and women today, with the happy result that a competitive negotiator is by no means always a male. She would like a big slice of that cake, too.

Competitive negotiating occurs most often when resources, power, prestige, or promotions—all chocolate cakes in their own right—are involved. It is outcome-based, and the relationship is often ignored. A Competitor corresponds to the Aggressive type of personality and is relished among those with finely tuned aggressive skills. This style is based on tough tactics, make-up-the-rules-as-you-go process, and a willingness to engage in protracted discussions. (Think NBA or AFL tirades.) Anyone living by the Accommodating or Amiable lifestyle will get suckered into competitive bargaining now and then but won't be comfortable or particularly successful at it. And Amiables cringe at the thought of jeopardizing a positive working relationship.

COMPROMISING

A *Compromising* negotiating style is characterized by each side making concessions and agreeing on the outcome. It is a blending performance, in which something is gained but can be considered to be a logical solution. A compromise would mean sharing the cake—but not necessarily equally. It's the old "You cut the cake, but I get first pick" game. Both parties come away with something; it may be called a win-win situation, even if it is a partial victory only. Compromisers are a little like the Expressive personality in that they are social folks who love to be included in decisions, and they usually like to discuss issues over food—like chocolate cake. They strive for smooth relationships and usually need a numbers guru to keep them on track, but may adopt the "get even" attitude if you mess with them too harshly.

Compromise is often considered to be a simple solution to simple problems. However, trouble sneaks in when one person begins by saying, "So, what are you prepared to give up?" forcing you to make the first concession. You have to evaluate the relationship in this case, because if it sounds like you are going to be giving up a larger portion of the cake, you may be better off in a more equitable or competitive style and not risk losing the potential gains as well as the relationship. The idea is not to be the first person to concede something.

Some basic homework is involved here, such as knowing both sides of the situation, being sure of what you are willing to lose and what you absolutely will not give up (many people call this their "walk-away" limit: You simply aren't going to walk away without a few bites of that yummy cake), and understanding that this is not a case of being even or getting even. You are looking for polite solutions to practical problems.

COLLABORATIVE

Collaboration is a useful style for creative problem solving within an organization when both the outcome and the relationship are important. This is similar to the compromising style, but a collaborative style works best when there is not enough for everyone, and an equitable solution must be worked out. It's a redefining rather than reorganizing, and it must be built on trust and honesty. This differs significantly from a competitive style, in which the goal is to get the biggest and best of that cake, including licking up all the crumbs. Collaborators want that cake to be shared equally by all, which makes them have a personality similar to the Analyzer, who would measure and divide even the crumbs to make sure each piece was exactly the same as all others. Collaborators need to understand the situation thoroughly, but they are usually willing to generate potential solutions, and, after they have all the facts, they are prepared to decide what works for everyone. Collaborating focuses on equal outcomes, which is often difficult to achieve, especially if there are 27 people and only one cake to be divided.

ACCOMMODATING

The final style is *Accommodating,* in which people simply give in to others' choices, preferring to relinquish gains to keep the relationship intact. You would give up the entire cake if it meant avoiding the loss of a friendship. Or you could walk off and pretend you didn't even know there was a luscious, mouth-watering cake sitting in the middle of the table. Accommodation is an avoidance technique and probably comes closest to the Amiable personality, which is the people pleaser and caregiver.

Reasons for negotiating in an Accommodating style include a plan to give in now with the hope of negotiating a future concession (you'd rather have a lemon meringue pie and will give up the cake to get a lion's share of the lemon in the future), to show respect for others, or simply because you can't stand an argument. One of the negatives of this style, however, is that sometimes other folks don't trust what they consider an easy win and wonder about your ulterior motives. This can be a trust-buster, not a relationship builder. Also, one who tends always to give in eventually may be squished by increasing numbers of competitive folks, thus spoiling any chances of ever getting any of the cake or pie.

Now that you have a solid idea of both your own personality style and the four common negotiating styles, we would like to think you still believe that "Knowledge is Power" and you are ready to dive into the working world. First, however, there is just a smidgen more research you need to do.

Five Important Questions

Before you begin any negotiation process, whether it be for a position or a raise or a project or even to wangle a desk near a sun-filled window, it helps to follow the basic formula taught to journalists the world over: Make a list labeled WHO? WHAT? WHEN? WHY? and HOW?

Who?

Determine as much as you can about the individual with whom you need to negotiate. You will establish some of the basics first:

1. Decision-making power: Does this person have the power to hire you? Or will he/she introduce you to the hiring manager after the interview?

2. Financial/personal motivation: Obviously, you want the best possible salary, with regular increases or bonuses, so we know your motivation. And we know that the company is going to try to get you for the least possible salary. But companies do have salary ranges and established pay schedules, so the motivation is to make the best of the situation and end up with an equitable and satisfactory result.

3. Gender: In the career counseling field, we call this one of the "isms." There are many isms in the working world, such as genderism, racism, sexism, ageism, culture-ism, size-ism, and any other prejudiced peccadillo humans come up with, all of which we consider to be silly and stupid and without any basis in fact—but they do exist. Moneyism exists as well: Women still make about 74 cents to the male $1 (see Appendix B). And yes, the glass ceiling exists in many companies, and certain positions (secretary, child care provider, nurse, and elder care provider, to name a few) are still considered beneath the dignity of most men to pursue. Enterprising women may

decide to take the entrepreneurial route, work in small businesses with mostly women hires, or simply stick around the corporate world and fight the ism issues from the inside. The suggestion here is to know with whom you will be negotiating, man or woman, and his or her individual style, and then to negotiate from strength of knowledge.

4. Culture/language: Different cultures have different customs, from body language and eye contact to speaking and language styles. The Japanese are quite successful at presenting an Amiable front but being powerful, no-nonsense Aggressive negotiators—with a smile. Other cultures have other personality styles unique to them. Fortunately, we are becoming such a diverse workforce that we are able to meet many individuals from all over the world, and, based on our communication skills, we can learn from each other. If you are going to be negotiating with someone from a different culture, please make sure you have a full understanding of how he or she will be handling the communication process.

5. Age: Ahhh, another ism, and a huge one. The magazines and newspapers are full of stories of workers in their 40s and 50s being let go (downsized, laid off, "this position is being eliminated," or whatever euphemism the company chooses to use) because their age is considered a detriment. "Hey, we can pay the same salary and get two young bucks right out of school, whose skills are sharper," the youthful owner of a computer business told me. Midlifers can argue or threaten lawsuit, but the company legal staff seems to have the company backsides covered, often by changing the title of the position. It happens, it's real, it's a problem, and it's tough to fight. When it comes to negotiating, however, age often is considered an advantage—and we suggest that if you are in an experienced age bracket (yes, many midlifers are getting fresh new doctorates and searching for exciting new careers), then brag about your extensive and finely honed skills, your flexibility, and dependability.

What?

What are you negotiating for? The list can go on for pages, because everything under the roof is considered negotiable, but here's a basic list:

1. Base salary, including time frame for raises, bonuses, merit pay, and a company car.

2. Health benefits, including medical, dental, visual, checkups, life/disability insurance, family plans, and copay rates.

3. Maternity/paternity leave and sick time.

4. Child care/personal time days.

5. Flex time and work-at-home days.

6. Retirement plans (yes, we know the life span of employees at one company is short these days, often less than 5 years, but we can dream, can't we?). Is there a defined benefit plan, 401K, and stock options?

7. A year's lease on a new BMW. (Don't laugh, it happens.)

8. Repayment of tuition loans.

9. Any perks involved (still dreaming here), such as company cars, spouse travel, discounts for merchandise, first-class accommodations on planes and in hotels, and use of company exercise facilities.

10. Education allowances for professional growth and advancement.

11. Updated equipment for you or your department. Safety issues.

12. Relocation may be down the road. Who pays those expenses? If you own a home, what happens if you can't sell it? If relocation is temporary, will the company pay? Some folks even ask for career transition services for the spouse or tuition help for their children's private schools.

In other words, think ahead and know exactly what you are negotiating for and what is important to you, and have as many facts and figures on hand as possible.

When?

Timing is important—and so is setting a time and sticking to it. Be prepared, however, to negotiate at a moment's notice. Some of the most important decisions are made not in somber offices in dulcet tones but when walking to the cafeteria or hanging out before a meeting—or on a golf course, in which case you'd better take up the sport if you want to score with the decision makers. If possible, set a time and place and honor the time commitment to the minute. And be ready to take breaks for cooling off or reanalyzing time if necessary.

Where?

As a prospective employee, you won't get the chance to choose the location, but if by chance you do, choose wisely: a quiet, comfortable room with no interruptions, phone calls, walk-ins, or food deliveries unless they are scheduled in advance. Many people tell me they'd also like to ban cell phones during these important meetings, but these are usually the same people who swear they simply cannot live without a phone attached to their ear and whose phones or pagers crackle like raucous crows during any solemn occasion.

Why?

Why are you going through this tedious exercise, and what do you stand to gain from it? Is the possible gain worth the extensive effort? If you are still committed after a full analysis of the why question, then go for it.

Negotiating a Starting Salary or Pay Raise

Pay is usually the most structured and most analyzed segment of the working world. It is connected to everything we do and is usually how we judge the value or worth not only of our work but of ourselves (and, unfortunately, of others). Sometimes, we have no opportunity to negotiate a salary pay raise, but because this is such an important area, we chose this as an example of using negotiating techniques.

Suggestions for Negotiating a Starting Salary

1. Know your market value and base requirements before you enter into a discussion. Finding out what your value is should be done ahead of time, so put your research hat back on for this one. Jump on the Internet (a list of Web sites for salary range comparisons is in Appendix C, and more are sprouting up daily) and check for your job description and area of the country. You will have to have a job title to conduct your search, so have several titles handy—what might be termed a customer service manager in one place may be an administrative supervisor in another.

   Also, have your minimum salary requirements in your head as well as your "walk away" number. Don't bother to negotiate if you know you need $40,000 to survive and you find positions offering $28,000. It's too big a gap. You need to start high—why not? You're a professional.

2. Research, research, research! One of your strongest, most highly developed talents will help you out here. How is the global economy and, in particular, the economy of the specific industry you are targeting? Do you feel the prognosis for this field is strong, positive, futuristic, or over the hill but ignoring the downturn signs? Now refocus on the company you are targeting. How is your prospective company doing financially? Big projects in the works, contracts looming rosy future? Or did they just miss or lose out on a big contract worth megabucks and have no other brainstorms in the pipeline?

   Can you find out if your company's budget has wiggle room or if all monies already have been allocated for the next year? Checking out Hoovers.com is a valuable exercise, if the company is large enough, and getting annual reports is a huge help, if you can decipher the mumbo jumbo of the fine print.

   Besides looking at the global and local outlook for your industry, you need to know that certain positions in your company have regimented pay scales and what slot you currently fill. Some positions simply receive an annual raise of 3%; other positions are the hot spots that offer a 30% raise as an incentive for the anticipated boom year. For example, human resources people tend to get the standard yearly increase, whereas an executive headhunter may get the serious bonus or salary increases because of current business goals or hiring targets you know nothing about.

3. The old negotiating axiom that "whomever mentions money first, loses" is still around. The trouble with this is that current hiring trends are for the HR person or the hiring manager to telephone you—it's called a "screening interview"—and ask what your salary requirements are. We suggest you try to stall, to get to an interview and be offered the position first, by saying, "My research indicates that a person with my experience and job title makes from $32,000 to $47,000, and my expectations are within that range." Substituting the word "expectations" for "requirements" lets them know where you stand. Just make sure you have that information firmly lodged in your brain.

The problem with this is that they often will push you for a figure. If you're fresh out of school, with no experience in the real world, you'll need to dance around this with a fast review of your skills and talents and your research results. Let them know you won't be interested in giving away those hard-won skills.

Companies say they ask for salary up front for two reasons: to screen out those whom they cannot afford and to see if your experience matches the company requirements. If you have worked for a significant salary, you are expected to have had more responsibility, and thus may be more attractive, if the salary numbers mesh.

So, here is the bottom line: Don't give a number, give a range. When they ask for a number, use the old psychology trick and answer a question with a question. A company rep may ask, "What salary are you expecting?" and you counter with, "What is the salary range for this position?" Don't haggle on numbers in a telephone interview; this is just a screening. You want to get into the interview and be offered the position before you get to the down-and-dirty dollar details.

4. There are other negotiable items. Flip back to the "WHAT" section for a list of all the potential items to negotiate. Just remember that the standard advice is to negotiate base salary first, and then to go for the goodies.

5. Accepting a job/salary offer: We have to slip back into gender-ese here, because men and women often react differently when offered a strong salary and a promising position. When a job offer comes in—and we're told it often comes by phone or mail—women tend to grab it as the offer stands and won't or don't want to negotiate. Men, with their finely tuned strong egos, easily think they may wangle more, so they ask to come in and discuss the numbers. Most of the time they end up with a better

package. Some researchers feel this is why women are paid less than men in many companies, because women won't go into the deal willing to negotiate for more base compensation. We don't know how much faith to put in this argument, but consider the facts: All the raises and bonuses come from starting salary, so this is the time to stick up for yourself. If women could forget their training to be accepting of what is offered and be willing to push for further negotiation, we might close the gender salary disparity more rapidly. Why not ask? All anyone can say is no.

Once a position is offered, you know they are interested in having you join their organization. They are now actively recruiting and are willing to make adjustments if that's what it takes to get you. If you are talking to a hiring manager, you have a good chance of improving your package. If you are talking to human resources, however, forget negotiating. Their job is to fill the position at the salary number the company gave them, and no changes will be discussed. It's now a take-it-or-leave-it proposition.

6. The offer is final, you want it—do you accept right away or delay? This is a standard question, but it can only be answered depending on your situation. If you have three other interviews pending, and they all sound promising, tell the company representative your situation and ask if you could respond to their offer within two to three days. Some career counselors will tell you that even if this is the best (or only) offer you've had, and you are excited about it, you always should wait at least one day to give them the "yes." We differ on this point. We think if you love the position and the company and feel there is room for growth—in other words, it's a very exciting proposition—why not accept on the spot? But don't stop job hunting until you receive the final contract and it verifies all the negotiated and agreed-on points and you have signed on all the many dotted lines.

If you are negotiating for a pay raise, there are some points to consider. Pay often is linked to the time you've remained in a position, and, assuming you are still breathing, performing reasonably well, and haven't piled up a lot of sick days or extra vacation time, you should receive regular raises, usually on an annual basis. Some companies put raises on a performance or outcome-based level, so you better produce or the one coming out—of the company organizational chart—is you. Although your performance may be terrific, you still may have to toot your own horn about it: Perhaps perfection is the norm in your workplace, in which case you'll have to stretch to get the regular yearly raises. Whatever the environment, you'll have to be able to report on exactly what you have done to boost the company's bottom line.

And remember, staying overtime doesn't count—you have to be able to prove your value in money saved, time saved, contracts brought in, or projects completed—and, if possible to document, exactly how much money you made/saved/created/found for the company. Bottom lines are the only lines that matter.

Also, when getting ready to present your case, don't compare yourself to anyone else, not anyone in your department or division or lunchroom or industry. Keep it strictly on a merit basis, perhaps after a big success or a good earnings report. Adopt the Analyst negotiating style: Present facts, remain unemotional, and ask for consideration. Then leave the room. You most likely won't get a quick answer, so hustle back to work and put it out of your head for now. We're told that with luck, you'll get an answer within 1 to 3 weeks.

The positives are easy—either you get the raise or you are told "soon" or "maybe later" and the work and respect level stays the same. A problem may arise, however, if you're turned down flat and either you or the boss gets upset. If you're upset, you can work or exercise it off and get back to the task at hand or quit. If the boss gets upset, let's hope he or she doesn't decide you are a malcontent or a slacker or someone who simply doesn't understand the current budget constraints or calls you the current dirty words, "not a team player." These are deadly words that can create a big negative in the work environment. Positives, always.

Many of the resources touting rules of negotiation advertise the process as a game, advising we should relish the challenges and opportunities for growth and learning, as well as the basic purpose: better financial compensation. Thinking of it as a game may take the emotion out of the process, which is good, but many professional advisers use warrior language, attitudes, and metaphors, which many people, particularly women, find uncomfortable.

We can overcome any of these hurdles, however, if we first remember that negotiations are an everyday part of our lives and should not be looked on as an alien concept. When negotiating for a new salary or a pay raise, it helps to think of negotiation as an orderly, progressive process, and we now understand both our own negotiating styles and those of others. If we are willing to be flexible to adapt to and meet each new challenge, we will be successful in helping move both ourselves and our company in a positive direction.

Isn't that the goal?

CHAPTER 12

Evaluating Job Offers

Take This Job and Love It

W ith perseverance, dedication, and a bit of serendipity, you will be offered a position that fits your talents and goals, both personal and financial. With even more of these, you will be offered a choice of potential careers. When this happens, let your feet return to earth, and then prepare yourself for some serious evaluations.

You may even be offered one of the common carrots offered to qualified job seekers these days, such as a signing bonus, a company car, incentives in the form of stock options (if not, you didn't major in computer science), end-of-year bonuses, or, if you are a real hot shot, monthly greens fees at Pebble Beach or tickets to the Winter Olympics.

Before you begin your evaluations of job offers—and yes, there will be several, at least, and they may even arrive on the same day—put away your trusty camera that has served you well in the previous chapters. It's time to develop those rolls of film, and then spread the colorful photos all over your dining room table. Choosing which one will be the full-color 16×20 enlargement, to be framed and hung in a place of honor beside your diploma, is your final decision.

The considerations include salary, opportunities for career longevity and advancement, the company culture, personal/family priorities, cost of living (especially if relocation is a potential decision), and then, simply, getting on with your life.

Salary

"Show me the money" is a current phrase, and, indeed, that's usually the first and primary number you need to see. You should have received a salary offer by the hiring person, which often comes in a fine-print contract offer in the mail a few days later. Read that print, and make sure everything that was agreed to is still part of the package.

Check out the numbers in the benefit package as well as other perks that were discussed in your negotiations. Some people even go so far as to have an attorney review the document, but surely you know that the company attorneys, who have written these contracts, have covered all the bases. You just need to make sure you're in the same ballgame.

Salary is a major concern for everyone, and it is the primary motivator. Compliments and nice offices and easy working conditions are lovely, but they don't put food on the table or the roof over your head. If you came out of school in the same financial shape as many students—close to penniless with loans that require immediate payments—your salary is going to be critical.

Think about the changes in your life. Getting that lovely diploma means you are now off the lists for receiving university discount books or inexpensive student rates at local restaurants; you are being bounced back into the full-price world again. And if you have been cruising along by shuffling debt from one credit card to another, you will discover that game is probably over, too. Goodbye to avoiding bills, hello to paying regularly. We hope you figured all this in before, or during, negotiations.

Career Longevity and Advancement

As you review your proposed contract, you are certain to discover that there is nary a word about career longevity or potential advancement. It may have been discussed in the hiring process, but no company is foolish enough to put that in writing. First of all, no one can predict what will happen to their company next week, much less in 1 or 5 or 10 years. Second, because employees tend to jump companies far more than in the past to seek more exciting and lucrative positions in other places, you may not want to be tied down, either. The word *tenure* is not, and never will be, in the business dictionary.

The only way you will have any idea about your potential is by the research you already completed on the companies you chose to apply to and interview. For instance, if you have a contract from a Fortune 500 company that has been around for 50 years, you might think a stable future is ensured. But if you read the newspapers and financial journals, you will realize big changes are happening. Entire manufacturing divisions are often being established in other countries, with people at all levels asked to move overseas to supervise or find another position. Buyouts, mergers, downsizes, and collapses are going on daily. No company of any size is immune to the economic forces or the world.

The same concept applies to small companies as well. Being bought out sometimes seems like a lifesaving dream, especially if the alternative is going under for the last time. As one frustrated job seeker reported, "The big fish are frantically gobbling up the small fish, and people working for the small fish are being tossed to the sharks." If you are signing on with a "small fish," know that changes can happen in a gulp, and you may be back in the job pond sooner than anticipated. Because you can't predict these things, go where your heart and head and intuition tell you to go, and keep flexibility as one of your most enduring personality traits.

As far as advancement goes, this is also up to you: Swim hard, work smart, be efficient, and make sure the important people know how extraordinarily capable you are. That's what creates faster movement and more exciting challenges.

Company Culture

You probably have a good idea about the environment of the companies you interviewed, and we hope you asked the human resource person—or the hiring manager or whomever gave you the job offer—if you could meet other people in your potential department. Seeing the size of your proposed location and learning the makeup and personalities of these people will give you a strong understanding of the culture. You will know immediately if you will be comfortable there or not.

We also suggest you try to talk to some other employees to try to gauge the big picture of what it's like to work there. We talked about these areas previously, aspects like to whom do you report, how is communication handled, what's the mission or vision of the company, and what about overtime and bonuses. Knowing the culture helps you make a solid decision.

Personal/Family Concerns

These are, or can be, major items of consideration. If you are footloose and fancy-free at the moment, only responsible for your own maintenance, you may not be overly concerned with where you land or the hours you will be required to work. But if you contemplate ever having a family or already have one, the picture becomes far more complicated. Schedules for working spouses, advancement issues (and potential requirements of relocating) for both of you, children's needs and schools, and quality of life are only tiny pieces of what needs to be considered here.

Our best suggestion is to make sure there is an ongoing and open communication between all parties involved, so the decision is a joint one. That's the only way it will work out best for everyone.

Cost of Living

The living costs differ from town to town, state to state, region to region, country to country. This is part of your initial homework when you researched companies, and we hope you kept this picture handy, ready for quick reference. A salary of $50,000 goes a lot farther in many inland areas of the country than it does along the coasts. From housing to groceries to public/private education for children to entertainment to restaurants, it all has to be factored in.

Get on With Your Life

Are you ready to select the best portrait of all, the one that has your personality, talents, skills, goals, and dreams in full living color? Can you match it to one of the positions offered to you? If not today, then soon. You will find an exciting new career, and with your excellent credentials and eagerness to join the real world of commerce, you will be joining millions of other doctoral graduates who have made the same leap and who are having a great time.

Don't look back: The future is looking too good.

Appendix A

Suggested Readings

Chapter 1: Assessing Your Academic Powers

Bolles, Richard Nelson. (1997). *What color is your parachute?* Berkeley, CA: Ten Speed Press.

Bolles, Richard Nelson. (1997). *The three boxes of life.* Berkeley, CA: Ten Speed Press.

Edwards, Paul, & Edwards, Sarah. (1996). *Finding your perfect work: The new career guide to making a living, creating a life.* New York: Putnam.

Konek, Carol Wolfe, & Kitch, Sally L. (1994). *Women and careers.* Thousand Oaks, CA: Sage.

Moreau, Daniel. (1996). *Take charge of your career: Survive and profit from a mid-career change.* Washington, DC: Kiplinger.

Chapter 2: Taking a Closer Look—Personality Profiles

Bates, Marilyn, & Keirsey, David W. (1978). *Please understand me.* Del Mar, CA: Prometheus Nemesis.

Carter, Carol, Kravits, Sarah Lyman, & Vaughn, Patricia Spencer. (1995). *The career tool kit: Skills for success.* Englewood Cliffs, NJ: Prentice Hall.

Clawson, James G., Kotter, John P., Faux, Victor A., & McArthur, Charles C. (1992). *Self assessment and career development* (3rd ed.). Englewood Cliffs, NJ: Prentice Hall.

Krueger, Otto, & Thuesen, Janet. (1992). *Type talk at work.* New York: Dell.

Myers, Isabel Briggs. (1980). *Gifts differing.* Palo Alto, CA: Consulting Psychologists Press.

Tieger, Paul D., & Barron-Tieger, Barbara. (1995). *Do what you are: Discover the perfect career for you through the secrets of personality type.* Boston: Little, Brown.

Chapter 3: Identifying Interactive Skills

Alessandra, Tony, & Hunsaker, Phil. (1993). *Communicating at work.* New York: Simon & Schuster.

Krannich, Ronald L., & Krannich, Caryl Rae. (1998). *The best jobs for the 21st century* (3rd ed.). Manassas Park, VA: Impact.

Lutz, William. *The new doublespeak: Why no one knows what anyone's saying anymore.* New York: HarperCollins.

Popcorn, Faith, & Marigold, Lyn. (1996). *Clicking.* New York: HarperCollins.

Warschaw, Tessa, & Barlow, Dee. (1995). *Resiliency: Bouncing back faster, stronger, smarter.* New York: Master Media.

Wendleton, Kate. (1997). *Targeting the job you want: For job hunters, career changers, consultants and freelancers.* New York: 5 O'Clock Books.

Chapter 4: Applying Your Skills to the Job Market

Bolles, Richard Nelson. (1997). *Job hunting on the Internet.* Berkeley, CA: Ten Speed Press.

Davidson, Jeff. (1999). *Market yourself and your career.* Holbrook, MA: Adams Media Corporation.

Dixon, Pam. (1998). *Job searching online for dummies.* Foster City, CA: IDG.

Graber, Steven. (2000). *The everything get-a-job book.* Holbrook, MA: Adams Media Corporation.

Graber, Steven. (Ed.). (2000). *Electronic job search.* Holbrook, MA: Adams Media Corporation.

Harkavy, Michael. (1990). *101 careers: A guide to the fastest growing opportunities.* New York: John Wiley.

Kador, John. (2000). *Internet jobs! The complete guide to finding the hottest Internet jobs.* New York: McGraw-Hill.

U.S. Department of Labor. (1998). *Occupational outlook handbook.* Indianapolis, IN: JIST Works, Inc. (also see stats.bls.gov/oco/ocoiab/htm)

Chapter 5: Investigating Popular Paths

Your best choice for researching this area is the Internet and interviewing directly with individuals working in foundations or serving on foundation boards. Resource books are either nonexistent or too well hidden to find.

Chapter 6: Exploring Entrepreneurial Options

Your local bookstore has a huge selection of entrepreneurial books. This currently is a hot topic, so you will find more resources than you can read in the next 2 months. Here are some good ones we have found.

Adams, Bob. (1996). *Small business start up: Your comprehensive guide to starting and managing a small business.* Holbrook, MA: Adams Media Corporation.

Adams, Bob. (1998). *Writing a business plan.* Holbrook, MA: Adams Media Corporation.

Applegate, J. (1998). *201 great ideas for your small business.* Princeton, NJ: Bloomberg.

Holtz, Herman. (1999). *The concise guide to becoming an independent consultant.* New York: John Wiley.

Levinson, Jay Conrad. (1994). *Guerilla advertising.* Boston: Houghton Mifflin.

White, Sarah, & Woods, John. (1997). *Do it yourself advertising.* Holbrook, MA: Adams Media Corporation.

Yarnell, Rene Reid. (1999). *The new entrepreneur.* Reno, NV: Quantum Leap.

Chapter 7: Recognizing Gender and Cultural Issues

Glass, Lillian. (1992). *He says, she says: Closing the communication gap between the sexes.* New York: Putnam.

Jamieson, K. H. (1995). *Beyond the double bind: Women and leadership.* New York: Oxford University Press.

Mann, Judith. (1994). *The difference: Growing up female in America.* New York: Warner Books.

Morrison, Ann. (1992). *The new leaders: Guidelines on leadership diversity in America.* San Francisco: Jossey-Bass.

Reardon, K. K. (1995). *They don't get it, do they? Communication in the workplace— Closing the gap between men and women.* Boston: Little, Brown.

Tannen, Deborah. (1994). *Talking from 9 to 5: How women's and men's conversational styles affect who gets heard, who gets credit, and what gets done at work.* New York: William Morrow.

Chapter 8: Networking

Butwin, Robert. (1997). *Network marketing.* Roseville, CA: Prima.

Kerr, Cherie. (1999). *Networking skills that will get you the job you want.* Cincinnati, OH: Betterway.

Kramer, Marc. (1998). *Power networking: Using the contacts you don't even know you have to succeed in the job you want.* Lincolnwood, IL: VGM.

Krannich, Ronald L., & Krannich, Caryl Rae. (1996). *Dynamite networking for dynamite jobs.* Manassas Park, VA: Impact.

Roe, Ann, & Youngs, Bettie B. (1989). *Is your "Net" working? A complete guide to building contacts and career visibility.* New York: John Wiley.

Vilas, Sandy, & Fisher, Donna. (1992). *Power networking: 55 secrets for personal and professional success.* Austin, TX: Bard.

Chapter 9: Writing Effective Résumés and Cover Letters

There are hundreds of résumé books in university and community bookstores, but these are the ones we felt to be particularly helpful. You will surely find many others as well.

Allen, Jeffrey. (1995). *The résumé makeover.* New York: John Wiley.

Corbin, Bill, & Wright, Shelby. (1995). *The edge résumé and job search strategy.* Indianapolis, IN: Beckett-Highland.

Grappo, Gary Joseph, & Lewis, Adele. (1998). *How to write better résumés.* Woodbury, NY: Barron's.

Wynett, Stanley. (1993). *Cover letters that will get you the job you want.* Cincinnati, OH: Better Books.

Yate, Martin. (1997). *Résumés that knock 'em dead.* Holbrook, MA: Adams Media Corporation.

Chapter 10: Perfecting Interview Skills

There are so many interview books on shelves, in your community library, and in university bookstores, that they practically leap off the shelves when you enter that aisle. These are some favorites.

Farr, J. Michael. (1995). *The quick interview and salary negotiation book: Dramatically improve your interviewing skills in just a few hours!* Indianapolis, IN: JIST Works, Inc.

Fein, Richard. (1996). *101 dynamic questions to ask at your job interview.* Manassas Park, VA: Impact.

Kanter, Arnold B. (1995). *Essential book of interviewing.* New York: Random House/ Times Books.

Medley, H. Anthony. (1993). *Sweaty palms: The neglected art of being interviewed.* Berkeley, CA: Ten Speed Press.

Porot, Daniel, & Haynes, Francis Bolles. (1999). *The 101 toughest questions . . . and answers that will win the job.* Berkeley, CA: Ten Speed Press.

Tullier, Michelle. (1999). *The unofficial guide to acing the interview.* New York: Macmillan.

Veruki, Peter. (1999). *250 job interview questions you'll most likely be asked.* Holbrook, MA: Adams Media Corporation.

Yate, Martin. (1999). *Knock 'em dead: Great answers to over 200 tough interview questions.* Holbrook, MA: Adams Media Corporation.

Chapter 11: Sharpening Negotiation Skills

Ilich, John. (1996). *Winning through negotiation.* New York: Macmillan/Alpha.

King, Julie Adair. (1995). *Smart woman's guide to interviews and salary negotiation.* CITY NJ: Carver.

Krannich, Ronald, & Krannich, Caryl Rae. (1998). *Dynamite salary negotiations: Know what you're worth and get it!* Manassas Park, VA: Impact.

Lewicki, Roy J., & Hiam, Alexander. (1997). *The fast forward MBA in negotiating and deal making.* New York: John Wiley.

Schapiro, Nicole. (1993). *Negotiating for your life: New success strategies for women.* New York: Henry Holt.

Chapter 12: Evaluating Job Offers

This is such a personal issue that it would be difficult to write about how to tailor every idea to each individual. Maybe that's why there are virtually no books on this topic. But, in the back of some negotiating books, there are sections discussing what is worth thinking about and discussing it with family members. You will have to use your detective skills (i.e., thumbing through the table of contents) to find this topic in other books.

Appendix B

Salary Comparisons of Women and Men[a]

Some professions obviously won't interest you, but it helps to be aware of general patterns. And who knows? Maybe you will decide you want a complete change of scenery and challenge.

Position	% Women	Women: Annual Salary	Men: Annual Salary	Women's Salary as % of Men's
Administrators: Education	59	37,960	57,770	66
Administrators, supervisors	60	28,912	35,308	82
Bartenders	54	15,236	19,708	77
Buyers: Retail, wholesale	48	30,680	33,644	91
Clergy	9	24,856	31,356	79
Computer operators	56	24,856	30,940	80
Computer programmers	28	37,180	45,968	81
Cooks	34	13,468	15,860	85
Corrections officers	24	26,468	29,692	89
Editors, reporters	44	32,032	42,224	76
Financial managers	52	36,556	52,884	69
Health care, medical managers	79	35,308	45,188	78
Health care technicians	39	25,272	30,576	83
Insurance adjusters, investigators	71	25,324	34,892	73
Lawyers	34	49,452	70,200	70
Management analysts	44	39,104	50,128	78
Marketing, advertising, public relations managers	38	39,468	58,656	67
Newspaper, magazine editors, reporters	44	32,032	42,224	76

a. Compiled by the staff of women.CONNECT.com using 1998 data from the Bureau of Labor Statistics, market analysts, and industry groups research.

Personnel, labor relations managers	64	38,844	49,244	79
Public administration officials	49	34,476	49,764	69
Purchasing managers	41	37,648	50,180	75
Real estate, sales	56	29,900	39,676	75
Security, sales, financial services	31	31,096	48,360	64
School counselors	68	35,828	37,700	95
Speech therapists	95	37,908	36,452	100
Teachers, K-high school	74	33,488	38,792	86

Here is the bottom line: In 1996, women were paid 74 cents for every dollar men received. The continued awareness and published numbers of this wage gap have escalated into an emotional and political reappraisal of all extended workplace issues, from gender discrimination to child care to family.

We urge both men and women to be aware of these issues both in your negotiating phase and when evaluating your final job offers.

Appendix C

Internet Resources[a]

Major Databases for Career Information and Posting Résumés

ajb.dni.us/	"America's Job Bank"; mostly government
Career.com	For computing, engineering, business development, and marketing
Careerbuilder.com	Salary calculator, salary survey, and key words
Careercast.com	You need to know what you are looking for
Careermag.com	Job openings, résumé bank, recruiter directory, job fairs, and news columns
Careermart.com/	Focus on advertising, sales, marketing, and public relations
Careermosaic.com	Mostly high tech and financial industries
Careerpath.com	Good site for college grads, relocation
Classifieds.yahoo.com/ employment.html	View by city and/or state
Coolworks.com/ showme/	Jobs at national parks, camps, cruises, or ranches—for those tired of stuffy ivory halls, desperately in need of fresh air and sunshine
Espan.com	Tech and nontech
Hotjobs.com	Stays current; many job postings
Jobweb.org/	For all graduates, not only recent ones. Links job seekers to job search information
Monster.com	Excellent for research and for "younger" workers
Nationjob.com/	Takes time; you can sign up to be notified of jobs
Net-temps.com	Not only temporary: part-time and full-time also
Occ.com	"Online Career Center"; high visibility, sales, and marketing
self-directed-search.com	John Holland's career profile
Topjobsusa.com	Managerial, technical, and professional opportunities

a. All URLs begin with "www," of course. And please remember: Sites change and new ones are constantly added.

Sites for Researching Company Web Pages, Financial Information, and Profiles

Bizweb.com	More than 30,000 companies and more than 190 links
companiesonline.com/	Excellent search engine
Forbes.com/tool/ toolbox/200best	Best of the "small fries"
Hoovers.com	Outstanding resource for everything—including getting names of competitors of any company; excellent site for doing research before your interviews
Inc.com500/	Fastest-growing companies
Jobsafari.com	Huge index; browse by alphabet/location

Sites for Salary Comparisons

Careers.wsj.com/	*Wall Street Journal* site—wide range of information; also link to "Salaries and Profiles" and "Salary Calculator"
Stats/bls/gov/	Bureau of Labor Statistics; career and job research
2.homefair.com/calc/ salcalc/html	Good comparisons by location
Wageweb.com	More salary research information

Sites for More Interview Information

collegegrad.com/intv/	More interview information
Datamasters.com/dm/ survey.html	Samples and information
dynastaff.com/tips.htm	Questions, answers, and extensive information
Sunfeatures.com/-jlk	1,001 job interview questions

Sites for Additional Résumé Ideas

Damngood.com	Can't lose with a title like this
Resumix.com/résumé/ resumeindex.html	Information about scanning
Resweb.com/	Large résumé postings and job databases; also offers lists of employers and additional resources. One of many sites to post résumés, but not a site for getting résumé help.
umn.edu/ohr/ecep/résumé	University of Minnesota "Resumania" site (all universities have similar info sites)

Hints

1. You should never have to pay to post your résumé on any site.

2. Some sites are not secure, and anyone with good or evil intentions can get their hands on nonsecured information. Be wise: Either don't post your résumé on unsecured sites or use only your first initial, and don't use your address or a private phone number. Only post your last name and a voice mail, fax, or e-mail address.

Sites for Nonprofit Information

Idealist.org/	Excellent database, access to free weekly e-mailed newsletter, and many links to resources
Jobs.pj.org	Nonprofit positions listed by region and category
Nonprofitcareer.com/	Job listings and job fair information
Nonprofits.org/	Mainly for access to organizations; if you know the organization or location, this will help
Tmcenter.org/	Nationwide listings for those seeking jobs in arts and humanities (see "NOC": Nonprofit Organization Classifieds)

Diversity Sites

Black-collegian.com/	Access to big job and résumé databases
Latinoweb.com/allusers.html	Listed alphabetically and free e-mail
saludos.com	General career information for Latinos

Sites for Women's Research/Information

WomenCONNECT.com	Compares men's and women's salaries by position for 78 professions
womenswire.com/work/?wcicareer	Excellent information, chat sights, and job database powered by monster board
Workingmother.com	Just as it says—for working mothers; getting good feedback

Fun Sites and General Information

Netnanny.com/allabout/ allabout.htm	This is the Net Nanny; you can lock out undesirable sites from your children
Queendom.com/test_frm.html	Personality and other tests on-line
Selfemployed.nase.org/NASE/	Information for becoming self-employed (NASE = National Association for Self Employed)
3.zdnet.com/yil/content/surfschool/ howto/howtotoc/html	Instructional site on how to surf the Net (provided, of course, you can get all that address typed in right)

Personality / Career Testing Sites

self-directed-search.com	A career search site
keirsey.com	Yields a personality profile with language and format similar to the MBTI. Many consider the Keirsey to be a quickie introduction to the Myers-Briggs.

Index

About the Authors

Jan Secrist, Ed.D., has extensive experience facilitating group seminars in written and verbal communication skills and personal development issues in business, military, and university settings. As a certified associate with Lee Hecht Harrison, a global career transition company, she coaches employees in résumé preparation, job search techniques, career patterns, and interview skills. Jan maintains a private practice for students exploring college/career options, and for 10 years she taught counseling and life span development classes in the master's counseling program at the University of San Diego. She is the author of *Tomboy Tales: Adventures of Midlife Mavericks,* stories of feisty, fun-loving wives, mothers, and career women, and coauthored *Secrets for a Successful Dissertation* (Sage). She has two other manuscripts in the development stage.

Jacqueline Fitzpatrick, Ed.D., is a member of the adjunct faculty for graduate students in the School of Education at the University of San Diego. She supervises and mentors student teachers in elementary schools throughout the San Diego area. Jacqueline earned her doctorate in Educational Leadership; her dissertation research was on the mentoring of professional women. She previously taught in elementary schools, has been an educational counselor to high school students, taught research techniques in the master's counseling program at the University of San Diego, coauthored *Secrets for a Successful Dissertation* (Sage), and currently is researching the challenges of midlife women struggling with various issues—aging parents, career options, grown but still dependent children, health concerns, personal and professional relationships, and retirement issues.